THE STORY OF
CIVILIZATION

VOLUME I
THE ANCIENT WORLD

Teacher's Manual

Copyright © 2016 TAN Books, PO Box 410487, Charlotte, NC 28241.

Cataloging-in-Publication data on file with the Library of Congress.

Illustrations by Chris Pelicano, Caroline Kiser

ISBN: 978-1-50510-570-4

Printed and bound in the United States of America

THE STORY OF
CIVILIZATION

VOLUME I
THE ANCIENT WORLD

Teacher's Manual

TAN

CONTENTS

A Word to the Teacher 7

Activity Materials at a Glance 13

Chapter 1: The Dawn of Civilization 31

Chapter 2: The Gift of the Nile 35

Chapter 3: Egypt in the Pyramid Age 41

Chapter 4: The Land Between Two Rivers 47

Chapter 5: Egyptian Empires 51

Chapter 6: Peoples of the Levant 55

Chapter 7: The God of Israel 59

Chapter 8: The Kingdom of David 63

Chapter 9: The Bearded Kings of the North 67

Chapter 10: The Splendor of Babylon 71

Chapter 11: The Rise of Persia 75

Chapter 12: People of the Isles 79

Chapter 13: The Founding of Greece 83

Chapter 14: Greek Mythology 87

Chapter 15: The Cradle of Democracy 91

Chapter 16: The Persian Wars 95

Chapter 17: Lovers of Wisdom 99

Chapter 18: Greek Against Greek 103

Chapter 19: Alexander the Great 107

Chapter 20: The Hellenistic Age 111

Chapter 21: Greek Science 115

Chapter 22: The Etruscans 119

Chapter 23: The City of Seven Hills 123

Chapter 24: The Punic Wars 127

Chapter 25: Greece and Rome Collide 131

Chapter 26: Marius and Sulla 135

Chapter 27: The Rise and Fall of Julius Caesar 139

Chapter 28: The Coming of Christ 143

Chapter 29: Fishers of Men 147

Chapter 30: Life Under the Julio-Claudians 151

Chapter 31: Five "Good" Emperors 155

Chapter 32: Collapse 159

Chapter 33: The Growth of the Catholic Church 163

Chapter 34: The Empire Divided 167

Chapter 35: In This Sign, Conquer 171

THE ANCIENT WORLD

HOW TO USE THIS TEACHER'S MANUAL

Teaching History

History is at the core of any classical education. Engaging in the study of history gives a context for the world in which we live. Learning the great triumphs and failures of generations before us helps mold the decisions we make today. When taught in an engaging way, a student can take the people and events of the past and relate them to their lives. It is an opportunity for the ultimate vicarious experience and it can create a spark that will light the way for the next generation to solve problems, make discoveries, invent wondrous things, and inspire greatness.

Teaching Using the One-Room Schoolhouse Model

The Story of Civilization is a wonderful text for teaching a single student or for teaching many students of varying grades all at one time. This text is designed to be used for grades 1–8.

If you are using this text with younger grades, you should revisit it again when the student is older. A classical education depends on laying a broad foundation at a young age that will be expanded upon later. Using *The Story of Civilization* twice will enhance the student's knowledge of history and allow for the addition of detail in later grades that was not committed to memory in early ones.

Using a schoolhouse model is not something seen in brick and mortar schools today, but it was the standard in the very recent past … and it worked. Some home schools utilize this method out of necessity or convenience, and some do so very intentionally because they find it to be a superior pedagogical method. Regardless of the reasoning, the one room schoolhouse model works and works well.

If you use the schoolhouse model, your older students might enjoy sitting in and following along in their own book while you read to the younger students. Older students then have the opportunity to review on their own. Going over Questions for Review as a group provides older students the chance to help younger students with forgotten facts, and provides younger students the opportunity to show off what they know. Impressing the parent/teacher is often not nearly as enticing as impressing an older sibling. Likewise, learning something for your own sake may not be as enticing as sharing what you have learned with someone else.

If you are only using this text with students of the same age, the schoolhouse model can still be of great benefit. A little healthy competition can bring many children out of their shells and provide incentive for paying attention.

Using this Teacher's Manual

This Teacher's Manual is meant to work in conjunction with the Activity Book that goes along with the *The Story of Civilization: Volume I*. The activities contained in this book are to be used after your student has completed each chapter of the text book.

The following is a list of sections you will find in this Teacher's Manual and the appropriate age range for each section:

QUESTIONS FOR REVIEW

This section is beneficial for the full range of elementary and middle school grades. For early elementary students, this section should be completed orally with lots of prompting and helpful hints. If you find the child struggling to come up with the answers independently, it may be most beneficial to both read the questions and provide the answers while engaging in discussion. *Mastery of the answers should not be expected at these young ages.* Exposure to the concepts is the key. For later elementary students, an oral evaluation is recommended. Expect most of the details to be provided by the student with minimal prompting. Oral answers should be given in complete sentences. For the middle school grades, a written evaluation would be ideal. Again, expect the student to provide most of the details. If you are teaching both elementary and middle school grades together, use the questions as an oral review for all, allowing the older students to aid the younger students with the details. Then, use the questions as a written review for the older students. At this point, expect well written responses since the questions have been reviewed orally.

NARRATION EXERCISES

This section is most beneficial for the elementary aged student. Ask the student to provide you with a brief summary of the chapter. For the early elementary grades, expect knowledge of the basic storyline and provide any details that the child has omitted. For later elementary grades, the story line should be supplied by the student. An example has been provided for each chapter. This is just an example, not something that needs to be duplicated exactly by the student. You may want to have older elementary students keep a written account of their own responses. If desired, the teacher can produce and keep a written account for younger students.

MAP ACTIVITIES

This section is beneficial for the full range of elementary and middle school students. It is meant to provide a visual reference for the locations in which the stories take place. It is helpful to make use of a world map from time to time to remind the students of the overall world placement of the events before honing in on the particulars of the exact locale. This teacher's manual provides directions for each map activity. The maps are located in the student's Activity Book under the chapter that corresponds with this text. You will find a map activity for almost every chapter.

ACTIVITY PROJECTS

There are a variety of Activity Projects found in this Teacher's Manual, each suited to different ages and interests. *Please note that not all of the activities should be completed for each chapter.* Choose the activities that will most engage your students, which will in turn fix the stories in their minds. Also note that a "Materials at a Glance" section has been added to the front of this manual so that you can gather your materials in advance without having to flip through each chapter. The possibilities of activities include:

COLORING PAGES

These are found in almost every chapter and correspond with the illustrations in the text book. Visual representation for each chapter helps the student identify the events more clearly. Some coloring pages are purposefully designed to be more elaborate than a traditional coloring page. The lines aren't as clean, and there is a lot more detail. This makes these coloring pages ideal for the full range of elementary students as well as middle school students. Especially in the early elementary years, it is helpful to give out the coloring page *before* you begin reading the chapter. Allowing the child to work on the coloring page while the chapter is read keeps idle hands busy and brings to life the stories they are hearing.

GAMES AND CROSSWORD PUZZLES

These are designed for students of all ages depending on the sort of activity it is. Activities include Word Searches, Cross Word Puzzles, Cryptograms, Double Puzzles, Mazes, Games, and even Magic Tricks. Some require turning to the Activity Book to locate, while others do not. When answers are needed they can be found in the corresponding chapters in the Teacher's Manual. Parents can use their own discretion on what their students can do.

CRAFT PROJECTS

These are mostly designed for the elementary school age student, although older students may find them fun as well. Gauge your student's interest level in doing the crafts. *Do not force these crafts on uninterested students.* History is supposed to be fun and these crafts are designed to support that idea, not become one more forced activity on top of all the other school work! Directions for each craft can be found under the appropriate chapter.

DRAWING PROJECTS

These are designed for older elementary and middle school aged students. They require a higher level of dexterity than most younger students can accomplish. Step-by-step directions with visual guides can be found in the Activity Book.

SNACK PROJECTS

Now, who doesn't love a good snack? And, in some cases a full meal? This section is for use by any age (including adults). The snack provides another link to the story studied and helps reinforce the chapter. Weeks or even months later when you ask for the story of Jericho and your student looks at you with a blank stare, you can say "remember the graham cracker walls and the gummy bears?" Just like that, the student can suddenly recount every detail.

SCIENCE PROJECTS

These are intended for upper elementary and middle school students. With a lot of help and supervision, early elementary students will also find these projects engaging. Again, the point is to reinforce the chapter and provide a hands-on project to help commit the stories to memory.

WRITING ASSIGNMENTS

There are a few writing assignments meant to make the student think about the chapter and put some of the information into their own creative wording. This is best accomplished with pen and paper by older students, but younger students may enjoy attempting them orally.

DRAMA PROJECTS

A great way to remember what you have read is to act it out. The student places themselves in the story and in doing so is more apt to remember the entire storyline.

THE 5 KEYS TO MAKING THE MOST OF THIS TEACHER'S MANUAL

1. *Remember, history is fun!* Keep the classroom mood light. Allow your students a little room to engage, ask questions, and participate in discussions. Students shouldn't read this subject in order to get it over with as quickly as possible. It's meant to lay a foundation for a love of learning. Whether your students are in elementary grades, middle school grades, or a mixture of the two, this text in meant to engage them in deep thought. They are challenged to open their minds and stretch their imaginations; to travel back in time to trace the origins of the human race and of the universe itself! Please make sure the journey is a fun one.

2. *DO NOT, under any circumstances, attempt to do all the activities in this book!* It's simply too much. Pick the activities that you think will be most beneficial for your students and do those. If you find a chapter or two in which you think all the activities are doable and you find yourself with extra time on your hands, go for it. If you find that one week a coloring page and word search were all that you could manage, don't beat yourself up. This curriculum is designed to be fun for both the student and the teacher.

3. *Be a passenger on the voyage.* If, as the teacher, you learn something new or are reminded of something that you almost forgot, let your students see that you too are growing in knowledge. Allow your own excitement of the stories to come out in your discussion with the students. The best way to engage your student is to be engaged yourself.

4. *Don't set the bar too high for younger students.* As parent-teachers we are often tempted to expect too much of our children because we know they are capable of it. If you are using this text with early elementary students you should revisit it when your children are older. Expose younger students to all that history has to offer, but don't try to drill every detail into them.

5. *If you have older students, let them take on some of the responsibility.* Let them look through the coming weeks and make a list of the activities they are most interested in. Allow them to list out and gather the supplies. If there are younger students in the classroom as well, allow the older students to pick out activities that they can help the younger students complete. Taking an active role in choosing the activities helps the student take ownership over what is learned.

Activity Materials at a Glance

Chapter 1

Craft Project 1: ARCHEOLOGY DIG

Materials:

- ☐ "Artifacts"—wooden beads, costume jewelry, plastic bugs, doll accessories, small plastic animals, (with explanation that although your cow is intact, you would actually be digging out bones), etc …
- ☐ Sand
- ☐ Water
- ☐ Used coffee grounds (not necessary, but add dimension to color)
- ☐ Baking pan
- ☐ String
- ☐ Colander
- ☐ Plastic baggies
- ☐ Marker

Craft Project 2: CLAY TABLET

Materials:

- ☐ 2 cups baking soda
- ☐ 1 cup corn starch
- ☐ 1 cup water
- ☐ Nonstick pot
- ☐ Glass baking dish or heat safe mixing bowl
- ☐ Kitchen or hand towel
- ☐ Food coloring (optional: orange and yellow work well)
- ☐ Rolling pin
- ☐ Popsicle stick

**Science Project: SHUKALLITUDA THE GARDNER'S
POTTED HERB GARDEN**

Materials:

☐ 4-8 used cans from canned foods
(assortment of sizes)
☐ Assorted paint colors (if you want to
paint your cans)
☐ Potting soil
☐ Pebbles

☐ Option 1: pre-grown plants OR option 2:
seeds. Choose your desired herbs such as
basil, parsley, thyme, cilantro, dill, oregano, mustard, sage
☐ Terracotta saucer (if using indoors)
☐ Drill

Chapter 2

Craft Project 1: A TUNIC FOR KING NARMER'S SOLIDER

Materials:

☐ A while pillow case or twin size sheet (depending on the size
of your child)
☐ Braided belt or rope belt

Craft Project 2: A SPEAR FOR KING
NARMER'S SOLDIER

Materials:

☐ Empty gift wrap roll
☐ Piece of black card stock paper
☐ Brown duct tape

Craft Project 3: A SHIELD FOR KING
NARMER'S SOLDIER

Materials:

☐ Cardboard
☐ Duct tape
☐ Markers
☐ Scissors

Craft Project 4: KING NARMER'S DOUBLE CROWN

Materials:

☐ Large piece of white craft foam (poster board may be used instead but is less pliable)
☐ Large piece of red craft foam (poster board may be used instead but is less pliable)
☐ Stapler
☐ Scissors
☐ Template in Activity book

Drawing Project: WRITE A MESSAGE IN HIEROGLYPHICS

Materials:

☐ Hieroglyphics template in Activity Book
☐ Drawing paper
☐ Pencil

Snack Project: NILE RIVER MELON KABOBS

Ingredients:

☐ Cantaloupe
☐ Honeydew melon
☐ Cubed cheese
☐ Wooden skewers

Chapter 3

Craft Project 1: PAPYRUS SCROLL—DJOSER'S DIRECTIONS TO BEGIN WORK ON HIS TOMB

Materials:

☐ Brown paper bag
☐ 2 wooden rods or knitting needles (each 9 or 10 inches long)
☐ Brown watercolor paint
☐ Stapler
☐ Black pen or marker

Craft Project 2: EGYPTIAN TOILET PAPER TUBE MUMMY

Materials:

☐ Toilet paper rolls
☐ White yarn
☐ Googly eyes
☐ Glue
☐ Tape

Drawing Project: SARCOPHAGUS

Materials:

☐ Drawing paper
☐ Pencil
☐ Eraser
☐ Colored pencils
☐ Template from Activity Book

Snack Project 1: EGYPTIAN HOT DOG MUMMY

Ingredients:

☐ 1-2 packages hotdogs
☐ 1-2 cans crescent rolls
☐ Mustard
☐ Pizza cutter

**Snack Project 2: THE GREAT PYRAMID
                    MARSHMALLOW TREAT**

Ingredients:

☐ 5 cups crispy rice cereal
☐ 4 cups of mini marshmallows
☐ 3 Tbsp. butter
☐ 1/2 tsp. vanilla

Chapter 4

Craft Project 1: MAKE A LAPIS LAZULI STONE

Materials:

☐ Smooth stone (find in a stream or at
  a pinch, or grab a non smooth stone
  from your backyard)
☐ Old toothbrush

☐ Blue paint
☐ Water sealer
☐ Small paint brush

Craft Project 2: SUMERIAN CLOCK

Materials:

☐ Paper plate
☐ Mini metal brad or paper fastener
☐ White paper
☐ Craft glue

☐ Construction paper (color of
  your choice)
☐ Markers (color of your choice)

**Craft Project 3: PAPER PLATE SNAKE WIND TWIRLER WHO ATE
                    GILGAMESH'S PLANT OF IMMORTALITY**

Materials:

☐ Paper plate
☐ Green, brown, black, any color washable paint for your snake
☐ Hot glue gun
☐ Red yarn
☐ Googly eyes
☐ Scissors

Chapter 5

Craft Project 1: HYKSOS CLOTHES PIN HORSE

Materials:

- ☐ 2 wooden clothes pins
- ☐ Brown paint
- ☐ Markers
- ☐ Yarn (brown, black, or tan)
- ☐ Template from Activity Book
- ☐ Scissors
- ☐ Glue

Craft Project 2: BRONZE SHIELD TO PROTECT THE ROYAL ARCHER

Materials:

- ☐ Cardboard
- ☐ Scissors
- ☐ Duct tape
- ☐ Bronze spray paint

Drawing Project: HOW TO DRAW A HORSE

Materials:

- ☐ Drawing paper
- ☐ Pencil
- ☐ Eraser
- ☐ Colored pencils
- ☐ Template from Activity Book

Chapter 6

Snack Project: CANAANITE FIG BARS

Ingredients:

CRUST AND TOPPING
- ☐ 3/4 cup butter, softened
- ☐ 1 cup packed brown sugar
- ☐ 1 1/2 cups all-purpose flour
- ☐ 1 tsp. salt
- ☐ 1/2 tsp. baking soda
- ☐ 1 1/4 cups quick-cooking oats

FILLING
- ☐ 1/4 cup granulated sugar
- ☐ 1 cup boiling water
- ☐ 9 oz dried figs, chopped
- ☐ 1/2 cup apple butter

Chapter 7

Craft Project 1: MOSES BASKET ON THE NILE

Materials:

- ☐ Paper plate
- ☐ White muffin liner
- ☐ Green construction paper
- ☐ Modeling clay
- ☐ Blue and brown markers
- ☐ Stapler

Craft Project 2: BURNING BUSH

Materials:

- ☐ Blue, green and brown construction paper
- ☐ Brown and green markers
- ☐ Red, yellow, and orange tissue paper
- ☐ Glue

Drawing Project: MOSES WITH HIS STAFF PARTING THE RED SEA

Materials:

- ☐ Moses drawing template from Activity Book
- ☐ Drawing paper
- ☐ Pencil
- ☐ Colored pencils

Snack Project: HOT MILK AND HONEY DRINK

Ingredients:

- ☐ 2 cups milk
- ☐ 2 tsp. honey
- ☐ 1/2 tsp. vanilla
- ☐ Pinch of cinnamon if desired

Chapter 8

Craft Project 1: TOILET PAPER / PAPER TOWEL ROLL DAVID AND GOLIATH

Materials:

- ☐ Template from Activity Book
- ☐ Colored pencils
- ☐ Toilet paper roll
- ☐ Paper towel roll
- ☐ Craft glue
- ☐ Scissors

Craft Project 2: TRUMPET AT JERICHO

Materials:

- ☐ Paper towel roll
- ☐ Markers
- ☐ Scissors
- ☐ 4 buttons
- ☐ Hot glue gun

Snack Project: GRAHAM CRACKER JERICHO

Ingredients:

- ☐ Sandwich bread
- ☐ Graham crackers
- ☐ Peanut butter or almond butter
- ☐ Gummy Bears

Chapter 9 ··

Craft Project 1: MAKE A SEA COW

Materials:

- ☐ Light grey modeling clay
- ☐ Markers

Craft Project 2: AQUEDUCT

Materials:

- ☐ Plastic straws
- ☐ Duct tape
- ☐ Small paper cups (bathroom cups)
- ☐ Objects from around the house to create slope for aqueduct
- ☐ Bowl

Chapter 10 ··

Craft Project 1: CONSTRUCT A ZIGGURAT

Materials:

- ☐ Empty boxes various sizes, (cereal, pasta, granola bar … etc), at least 4
- ☐ Yellow or tan construction paper
- ☐ Tape
- ☐ Glue
- ☐ Markers

Craft Project 2: GATES OF BABYLON

Materials:

- ☐ Large cardboard shipping box
- ☐ Blue, yellow, and orange paint
- ☐ 2 paper plates
- ☐ Brown, orange yarn
- ☐ Markers
- ☐ Super glue

Chapter 11

Activity Project: VANISHING ARMY TRICK

Materials:

- ☐ 3 pieces of paper, two the same color
- ☐ Ruler
- ☐ Pencil
- ☐ Scissors
- ☐ Glue stick
- ☐ Scotch tape
- ☐ Army template in Activity Book
- ☐ A glass

Craft Project: MAKE A PERSIAN RELIEF SCULPTURE

Materials:

- ☐ Bar of unused soap
- ☐ Soap carving pattern template in Activity Book
- ☐ Carving tools (these can be as simple as fork, plastic knives, and toothpicks, or can be true tools if you have them)

Chapter 12

Craft Project: CREATE A FRESCO

Materials:

- ☐ Plaster of Paris
- ☐ Plastic plate
- ☐ Paint
- ☐ Paint brushes
- ☐ Tooth picks

Chapter 13

Craft Project 1: DAEDALUS AND ICARUS SPOON PEOPLE

Materials:

- ☐ 2, 10-12 inch wooden spoons
- ☐ Templates from Activity Book
- ☐ Craft feathers
- ☐ Craft glue
- ☐ Markers
- ☐ Googly eyes
- ☐ Hot glue

Craft Project 2: TROJAN HORSE

Materials:

- ☐ Template from Activity Book
- ☐ White card stock paper
- ☐ Markers
- ☐ Glue stick
- ☐ Clear tape

Chapter 14

Craft Project 1: MAKE POSEIDON'S TRIDENT

Materials:

- ☐ Wrapping paper tube
- ☐ 12 x 12 cardboard (does not have to be exact)
- ☐ Duct tape
- ☐ Aluminum foil
- ☐ Scissors
- ☐ Template in Activity Book

Craft Project 2: GREEK ACTOR'S MASK

Materials:

- ☐ Paper plate
- ☐ Yarn (color for hair and / or beard)
- ☐ Hot glue
- ☐ Flesh tone paint
- ☐ Fine tip markers
- ☐ Popsicle stick

Chapter 15

Craft Project: SPARTAN SHIELD

Materials:

- ☐ 12 in diameter circular piece of cardboard (frozen pizza bottom works well)
- ☐ 10 in x 2 in strip of cardboard
- ☐ Duct tape
- ☐ Gold paint
- ☐ Black marker

Chapter 16

Craft Project: A THRONE FOR KING XERXES

Materials:

☐ Dining chair
☐ Cardboard … lots and lots of cardboard … several cardboard boxes (grocery stores often have extra boxes they want to get rid of)
☐ Gold spray paint
☐ Hot glue
☐ Construction paper or craft jewels
☐ Duct tape
☐ Plastic table clothes (or another suitable covering for a large spray paint area)

Drawing Project: GREEK WARSHIP

Materials:

☐ Drawing paper
☐ Pencil
☐ Eraser
☐ Colored pencils
☐ Template from Activity Book

Chapter 17

Craft Project 1: SOCRATES, PLATO, AND ARISTOTLE SPOON PEOPLE

Materials:

☐ 3 10-inch wooden spoons
☐ Templates from Activity Book
☐ Colored pencils
☐ Markers
☐ Googly eyes (if desired)
☐ Hot glue gun

Craft Project 2: CREATE YOUR OWN CHALKBOARD FOR WRITING OUT FAMOUS ARISTOTELIAN QUOTES

Materials:

☐ Old picture frame
☐ 1/4" thick hard board cut to fit frame
☐ Primer
☐ Chalkboard paint
☐ Chalk
☐ Activity Book page

Chapter 18 ···

Snack Project: GRAHAM CRACKER PARTHENON

Ingredients:

- ☐ Graham crackers
- ☐ Peanut butter or icing
- ☐ Pretzel twists (the thicker kind, can be found in the honey wheat)
- ☐ Full size marshmallows
- ☐ Candies for decorating if desired

Chapter 19 ···

Craft Project 1: MAKE ALEXANDER THE GREAT'S HOBBY HORSE

Materials:

- ☐ 3 foot long wooden dowel
- ☐ Poly-fil
- ☐ Old black sock (Dad's work best because they're bigger)—one with a different colored toe it will work best
- ☐ Square of black felt
- ☐ Square of pink or red felt
- ☐ Square of white felt
- ☐ Fabric glue
- ☐ Knitting needle
- ☐ Brown yarn, white yarn, red yarn (Whatever color you want for mouth, nose, and mane)
- ☐ Scissors
- ☐ Two buttons (if desired)
- ☐ Hot glue gun

Craft Project 2: SPEARS FOR ALEXANDER'S PHALANX

Materials:

- ☐ 1 Empty gift wrap roll (1 roll makes 2 spears)
- ☐ Piece of black card stock paper
- ☐ Brown duct tape

Chapter 20 ···

Craft Project: PHAROS LIGHTHOUSE

Materials:

- ☐ Colored pencils
- ☐ 12 oz solid white styrofoam cup
- ☐ Small empty glass baby food jar
- ☐ Flameless (battery operated) tea light

Chapter 21

Craft Project 1: PAPER MACHE GLOBE

Materials:

- ☐ Flour and water (Paper Mache glue)
- ☐ Round balloon
- ☐ Newspaper strips
- ☐ Paint (green, brown, blue, white, yellow)
- ☐ Paintbrushes
- ☐ Globe or atlas

Craft Project 2: ARCHIMEDES SCREW

Materials:

- ☐ Empty plastic water bottle
- ☐ Sharp knife (for adult use only)
- ☐ Tack
- ☐ Hole punch
- ☐ Unsharpened pencil
- ☐ Clear packing tape (or other strong tape ... not a big deal if it isn't clear)
- ☐ 12 oz glass
- ☐ Piece of card stock paper
- ☐ Crispy rice cereal

Science Project: EUREKA! WATER DISPLACEMENT

Materials:

- ☐ Graduated cylinder or other means of measuring in milliliters (a newborn bottle will work)
- ☐ Food scale (something that weighs in grams)—in the absence of a scale, choose objects that you can look up the weight.
- ☐ Water
- ☐ 3-5 similar sized objects (maybe a penny, piece of aluminum foil wadded up, pebble, small piece of mulch ... whatever you have handy).
- ☐ A calculator

Chapter 22

Craft Project: ETRUSCAN GOLDEN BRACELET

Materials:

- ☐ Toilet paper tube
- ☐ Gold acrylic paint
- ☐ Paint brush
- ☐ Glue
- ☐ Aluminum foil
- ☐ Craft sand (if desired)

Craft Project 2: HOMEMADE BOXING GLOVES

Materials:
- ☐ Old pair of mittens or socks
- ☐ Thin foam
- ☐ Duct tape
- ☐ Scissors

Chapter 23

Drawing Project: ITALY

Materials:
- ☐ Drawing paper
- ☐ Pencil
- ☐ Eraser
- ☐ Colored pencils
- ☐ Template from Activity Book

Chapter 24

Drawing Project 1: ADD SICILY TO YOUR MAP
FROM CHAPTER 23

Materials:
- ☐ Drawing paper
- ☐ Pencil
- ☐ Eraser
- ☐ Colored pencils
- ☐ Template from Activity Book

Drawing Project 2: WAR ELEPHANT

Materials:
- ☐ Drawing paper
- ☐ Pencil
- ☐ Eraser

Snack Project: CHOCOLATE PEANUT ELEPHANT EARS

Ingredients:

- ☐ 1 pkg. puff pastry (there are 2 sheets / package)
- ☐ Flour (for coating work surface)
- ☐ 1 egg
- ☐ 1 tbs. water
- ☐ 1/2 cup mini chocolate chips
- ☐ 1/4 cup crushed peanuts (more if desired)
- ☐ Parchment paper

Chapter 25

Activity Project: MANIPLE VS. PHALANX CHECKERS

Materials:

- ☐ Activity Book pages for game board and game pieces
- ☐ Coloring pencils
- ☐ Scissors
- ☐ Tape

Craft Project 1: WALKING STICK FOR THE OLD MAN WHO FACED THE ARMY

Materials:

- ☐ Solid wood stick appropriate for the height of the student
- ☐ Sanding paper
- ☐ Drill
- ☐ Leather cord
- ☐ Craft beads for decoration

Craft Project 2: MAKE A HAMMER TO REPRESENT MACCABEUS

Materials:

- ☐ Empty small oatmeal container (either cylinder or box will work here)
- ☐ Paper towel tube
- ☐ Duct tape
- ☐ Primer paint / white paint
- ☐ Silver or grey paint
- ☐ Brown paint
- ☐ Leather cord
- ☐ Hot glue gun
- ☐ Pencil
- ☐ Xacto knife

Chapter 26

Drawing Project: EAGLE'S HEAD

Materials:

- ☐ Drawing paper
- ☐ Pencil
- ☐ Eraser
- ☐ Colored pencils
- ☐ Template from Activity Book

Snack Project: GAIUS MARIUS EAGLE'S EGGS IN A NEST

Ingredients:

- ☐ 1 package semi-sweet or milk chocolate chips
- ☐ 1/2 cup peanut butter
- ☐ 4 cups chow mein noodles
- ☐ 1 package jelly beans

Chapter 27

Craft Project: MAKE A COBRA

Materials:

- ☐ Construction paper in the colors you want for your snake.
- ☐ Stapler or clear tape
- ☐ Googly eyes
- ☐ Craft glue
- ☐ Small piece of red construction paper (for tongue)
- ☐ Plastic straw

Chapter 28

Craft Project 1: NATIVITY STAINED GLASS

Materials:

- ☐ Template from Activity Book
- ☐ Black construction paper
- ☐ Tape
- ☐ Scissors
- ☐ Tissue paper in various colors
- ☐ Contact paper

Chapter 29

Craft Project: FISHING POLE—FISHERS OF MEN

Materials:

- ☐ Template from Activity Book
- ☐ 18 inch stick
- ☐ Scissors
- ☐ Colored pencils
- ☐ Tape
- ☐ Hole punch
- ☐ 18 inch piece of string

Science Project: COLORING THE WORLD:
THE SPREAD OF CHRISTIANITY

Materials:

☐ Milk
☐ Pie plate
☐ Food coloring

☐ Dish soap
☐ Cotton swab

Chapter 30

Craft Project: LAUREL WREATH FOR AUGUSTUS CAESAR

Materials:

☐ 2 plastic headbands
☐ Green construction paper

☐ Hot glue
☐ Scissors

Chapter 31

Craft Project: WILD BEASTS AT THE COLOSSEUM—LION

Materials:

☐ Paper plate
☐ Orange paint
☐ Yellow paint

☐ Googly eyes
☐ Black marker
☐ Scissors

Chapter 32

Craft Project 1: ANIMAL SKIN VEST FOR A BARBARIAN

Materials:

☐ Paper grocery bag
☐ Scissors
☐ Oil pastel paints or markers

☐ Paint brush (if applicable)
☐ Craft faux fur (if desired)
☐ Hot glue gun (if applicable)

Craft Project 2: THE CROWN OF THE CHRISTIAN MARTYRS

Materials:

☐ Red or white 9 in diameter paper plate
☐ Red crayon or marker if using white
     paper plate
☐ Scissors
☐ Hot glue
☐ Craft gems

Chapter 33

Craft Project: CATHOLIC CHURCH AND ROMAN EMPIRE TREES

Materials:

- ☐ Templates from the Activity Book
- ☐ 1 empty toilet paper roll
- ☐ Grey and brown crayons
- ☐ Green paint
- ☐ Tape
- ☐ Scissors
- ☐ Paint brush

Chapter 34

Craft Project 1: BOW AND ARROW THAT DOESN'T KILL ST. SEBASTIAN

Materials:

- ☐ Hardwood stick of appropriate length for the student.
- ☐ Knife / chisel (handle with care!)
- ☐ Sandpaper
- ☐ Rubber bands
- ☐ Thin wooden dowel (about the thickness of a pencil)
- ☐ Pencil eraser tops
- ☐ Hot glue

Chapter 35

Craft Project: CHI-RHO SHIELD CONSTANTINE'S DREAM

Materials:

- ☐ Cardboard
- ☐ Duct tape
- ☐ Red paint
- ☐ Paint brush
- ☐ Scissors

Snack Project: **EDICT OF MILAN FEAST**
CELEBRATION POUND CAKE WITH STRAWBERRIES

Ingredients:

☐ 1 cup butter, softened
☐ 3 cups sugar
☐ 6 eggs
☐ 3 cups all-purpose flour
☐ 1/4 tsp. baking soda
☐ 1/4 tsp. salt
☐ 1 cup sour cream
☐ 1 tsp. vanilla extract
☐ 1/2 tsp. almond extract
☐ Confectioners' sugar
☐ Baking spray

CHAPTER 1
The Dawn of Civilization

QUESTIONS FOR REVIEW:

1. **What are scientists called who study the people of the past?**

   Archaeologists

2. **What are some signs of a people becoming civilized, or developing a civilization?**

   Farming, building cities, and the development of the written word, as well as working with metal, training animals, and making pottery.

3. **What is the name of the dirt from the riverbed that helped with farming because it is so rich in nutrients?**

   Silt

4. **What were the people called who traveled up and down rivers trading goods?**

   Merchants

5. **Describe several ways the written word changed the way people lived.**

   It allowed them to trade more easily because they could keep track of things. It also allowed ideas to be passed down from one generation to the next, as well as stories.

NARRATION EXERCISES:

Nomads

These early people did not live in one place. Instead, they roamed the earth searching for food and sleeping in caves, tents, or under the open sky. They fed themselves by collecting fruits and nuts, or by hunting wild animals. When the food ran out in one place they gathered up everything they had and moved to another. They knew very little about the world around them, like why it got dark at night or what plants were safe to eat.

Shukallituda the Gardener

This Sumerian gardener had trouble growing crops because of the wind and sun. He had the idea to plant trees around his garden to protect his crops from the elements. After this, Shukallituda's garden blossomed with all sorts of green plants.

Activity Projects

CRAFT PROJECT 1: ARCHAEOLOGY DIG

Materials:
- ☐ "Artifacts"—wooden beads, costume jewelry, plastic bugs, doll accessories, small plastic animals, (with explanation that although your cow is intact, you would actually be digging out bones), etc …
- ☐ Sand
- ☐ Water
- ☐ Used coffee grounds (not necessary, but add dimension to color)
- ☐ Baking pan
- ☐ Yarn
- ☐ Tape
- ☐ Tape
- ☐ Large spoon or shovel
- ☐ Plastic baggies
- ☐ Marker

Directions:
1. Make your dig mixture. Fill your pan about 3/4 full with sand (and coffee grounds if you're using them). Add a little water gradually until your mixture becomes slightly damp.

2. Bury your artifacts randomly around in your pan.

3. Pack mixture down around the artifacts.

4. Using your yarn and tape, make a grid over your baking pan. Label each of the quadrants with a number (for example: if you are using a 9 x 13 pan, a 3 x 4 grid should work well).

5. Have your child excavate your sand mixture with a large spoon or shovel one quadrant at a time into your colander.

6. As your child finds artifacts, have him/her put them in baggies and label them according to which quadrant they were found in.

7. Enjoy!

CRAFT PROJECT 2: CLAY TABLET

Materials:
- ☐ 2 cups baking soda
- ☐ 1 cup corn starch
- ☐ 1 cup water
- ☐ Non-stick pot
- ☐ Glass baking dish or heat safe mixing bowl
- ☐ Food coloring (optional: orange and yellow work well)
- ☐ Kitchen or hand towel
- ☐ Rolling pin
- ☐ Popsicle stick

Directions:

1. Place 2 cups of baking soda, 1 cup of cornstarch, and 1 cup of water in a non-stick pot.
2. Cook over medium heat, stirring continuously until the mixture is lump free and the consistency of mashed potatoes. If using food coloring, add it to your mixture now.
3. Place mixture in your glass baking dish or heat safe mixing bowl.
4. Soak your hand towel and ring out.
5. Place hand towel over mixture and allow to cool.
7. Use a rolling pin to roll out your modeling clay, or just use your hands to form desired shape and size (remember, it doesn't need to be a perfect rectangle).
8. Use your popsicle stick to make marks in your clay.
9. Allow your clay to harden 12-24 hours.
10. Enjoy!

COLORING PAGES

Merchants (*Activity Book page 5*)
Color the picture of the merchants trading by the river.

SCIENCE PROJECT: SHUKALLITUDA THE GARDNER'S POTTED HERB GARDEN

Materials:
- ☐ 4-8 used cans from canned foods (assortment of sizes)
- ☐ Assorted paint colors (if you want to paint your cans)
- ☐ Option 1: pre-grown plants OR option 2: seeds. Choose your desired herbs such as basil, parsley, thyme, cilantro, dill, oregano, mustard, sage
- ☐ Pebbles
- ☐ Potting soil
- ☐ Terracotta saucer (if using indoors)
- ☐ Drill

Directions:
1. Thoroughly clean out your cans and paint various colors if desired.
2. Use a drill with a small drill bit to make 8 holes in the bottom of each can.
3. Place pebbles in the bottom of each can.
4. Place potting soil in each can.
5. Place pre-grown herbs or seeds in potting soil.
6. Water herbs.
7. If keeping indoors, place cans together in terracotta saucer and place saucer near a window with lots of sunshine.
8. If using outside, place the herbs where they will get enough sun.
9. Water according to the directions on herbs.
10. Now is a great time to intersect science with history and do a lesson on plant growth.
11. Enjoy!

CHAPTER 2
The Gift of the Nile

QUESTIONS FOR REVIEW:

1. **Who was King Narmer?**

   He is considered the first king, or pharaoh, of Egypt after he united Upper and Lower Egypt.

2. **Why is the Nile River so important to the Egyptians?**

   Most of Egypt is comprised of desert lands which get almost no rainfall. The Nile is the only source of water, so all Egyptians must live near it. The Nile helps with farming, trading, bathing, and many other important practices key to the Egyptian people's survival.

3. **What did Narmer wear as a sign of a unified Egypt?**

   He wore the double crown of Upper and Lower Egypt. Upper Egypt had a white crown, while lower Egypt had a red crown.

4. **Who created the first form of writing amongst the Egyptians, known as hieroglyphics?**

   The priests of the Egyptian gods.

5. **What is a shaduf?**

   A simple bucket on a lever which draws water from the river and irrigates crops.

NARRATION EXERCISES:

King Narmer

He was the great king, or pharaoh, of the southern kingdom of Egypt (Upper Egypt). He rode off to conquer the northern kingdom (Lower

Egypt) and won, thus forming a unified Egypt. To symbolize this unification he wore the double crown, which was comprised of the white crown of Upper Egypt, and the red crown of Lower Egypt. For this, Narmer is considered the first pharaoh of Egypt.

Upper and Lower Egypt

Egypt, before 3100 B.C., was divided up into two parts. But these kingdoms were confusing. Upper Egypt was actually in the south, and Lower Egypt in the north. This was because they named their regions based on their positions in regards to the Nile River. Upper Egypt was comprised of hills and highlands, and so the Nile was "up" in this region, while Lower Egypt was where the Nile emptied "down" into the Mediterranean Sea.

Activity Projects

MAP ACTIVITY: LOWER AND UPPER EGYPT *(Activity Book page 7)*

1. Locate Upper Egypt (note this is south of Lower Egypt) on the map and draw a white crown. This is the crown of King Narmer, the great king of the south.
2. Locate Lower Egypt on the map and draw a red crown. This was the crown of the king of the north.
3. In the middle of Lower and Upper Egypt draw a red crown atop a white crown and write "King Narmer" symbolizing that Upper and Lower Egypt are now united under king Narmer.
4. Locate the Nile River and trace it in blue.

COLORING PAGE

Narmer *(Activity Book page 9)*

Color the picture of the first pharaoh, Narmer, of a united Egypt.

CRAFT PROJECT 1: A TUNIC FOR KING NARMER'S SOLIDER

Materials:
- ☐ A white pillowcase or twin sized sheet (depending on size of child)
- ☐ Braided belt or rope belt

Directions:
1. Cut head and arm holes in the pillow case or cut head hole in the center of the sheet and cut to proper length.
2. Use the braided belt or rope belt to tie around the middle.
3. Enjoy!

CRAFT PROJECT 2: A SPEAR FOR KING NARMER'S SOLDIER

Materials:
- ☐ Empty gift wrap roll
- ☐ Piece of black card stock paper
- ☐ Brown duct tape

Directions:
1. Cut the tip of your spear (tear drop shape) from the black card stock.
2. Cut a 1/2 inch slit in the end of your gift wrap roll and slide the spear tip into place.
3. Use duct tape to secure your spear tip to its handle.
4. Enjoy!

CRAFT PROJECT 3: A SHIELD FOR KING NARMER'S SOLDIER

Materials:
- ☐ Cardboard
- ☐ Duct tape
- ☐ Markers
- ☐ Scissors

Directions:
1. Cut your shield to desired size from the cardboard.
2. Cut a 6 in x 2 in strip of cardboard and duct tape it to the back of your shield for the handle.
3. Use markers to decorate your shield.
4. Enjoy!

CRAFT PROJECT 4: KING NARMER'S DOUBLE CROWN

Materials:
- ☐ Large piece of white craft foam (poster board may be used instead but is less pliable)
- ☐ Large piece of red craft foam (poster board may be used instead but is less pliable)
- ☐ Stapler
- ☐ Scissors
- ☐ Template in Activity book *(Activity Book page 11–13)*

Directions:
1. Use the template from the activity book for a guide of the shape of each piece for the crown (white and red). This is not to scale. You will need the white piece for the crown to be about 10 inches tall and the red piece to be slightly taller.
2. Cut your white and red foam to the proper shape / size.
3. Measure the red piece to fit around the child's head and staple in place.
4. The tall section of the red piece is the back of the crown to go on the backside of the child's head.
5. Staple the white piece inside the front of the crown (opposite the tall section of the red piece).
6. Cut a 1 inch x 8 inch strip of red foam and wind it around itself so it will curl a bit. Staple one end in the bottom center of the white piece so that it curls at the top.
7. Enjoy!

DRAWING PROJECT: WRITE A MESSAGE IN HIEROGLYPHICS

Materials:
- ☐ Hieroglyphics template in Activity Book *(Activity Book page 15)*
- ☐ Drawing paper
- ☐ Pencil

Directions:
1. Have your child write a message in hieroglyphics.
2. Write a message for your child in hieroglyphics.
3. Decipher your child's message and ask your child to decipher yours.
4. Enjoy!

SNACK PROJECT: NILE RIVER MELON KABOBS

Ingredients:
- ☐ Cantaloupe
- ☐ Honeydew melon
- ☐ Cubed cheese
- ☐ Wooden skewers

Directions:
1. Cut melon into cubes.
2. Place melon and cheese on wooden skewers.
3. Enjoy!

CHAPTER 3
Egypt in the Pyramid Age

QUESTIONS FOR REVIEW:

1. **What is a dynasty?**

   A family who rules the kingdom.

2. **Describe how Imhotep came up with the idea of creating the first step pyramid.**

   He was already familiar with the mastabas, which were small, rectangular buildings where the dead pharaohs were buried underneath. He had the idea to stack mastabas on top of each other, each smaller than the one below it, which formed the step pyramid.

3. **What was the name of the book where the Egyptian priests kept track of the rituals for burying a pharaoh?**

   The Book of the Dead.

4. **What did the nomarchs do in ancient Egypt?**

   They were governors and ruled various regions of the kingdom. They collected taxes and enforced the pharaoh's decrees.

5. **How long was Pepi II's long reign?**

   Ninety-four years!

NARRATION EXERCISES:

Pyramids

These giant structures were used as tombs for the pharaohs after they had died. They took many years to construct and were first designed by Imhotep. The pyramids were often full of dead ends, false doors, and hidden passages because tomb robbers would try to break into them and steal the treasure buried with the pharaoh. The pharaohs were mummified before being buried in the pyramids because it was believed they would only experience peace in the afterlife if their body was preserved.

Egyptian Afterlife

The rites surrounding the death of a pharaoh were the most important. When a pharaoh died, his body underwent a complex process of preparation for mummification. A mummy is a body that has been treated so it does not decay. It was believed that the king's departed soul would have peace so long as the body was preserved. The Egyptian priests were in charge of carrying this out. The priests wrote a book called the Book of the Dead that explained all these rituals.

In the beginning, the Egyptians believed only the pharaoh's soul was privileged enough to enjoy rest after death, while the souls of common people went down to a dark underworld. But gradually Egyptians came to accept that anybody could enjoy peace in the next life if they were righteous. The Egyptians believed that at death, a person's soul was weighed in a scale against a feather. If they had done no evil, they would be admitted into eternal happiness.

Activity Projects

MAP ACTIVITY: EGYPTIAN PYRAMIDS *(Activity Book page 17)*

1. Locate the Nile River and trace it in blue. Draw arrows running parallel with the Nile going in both directions, up and down the Nile. This is to demonstrate that the Nile was like a main road providing merchants and messengers with a means of travel to other parts of Egypt.

2. Just north of Memphis, draw a six-step pyramid. This is the famous step pyramid of Djoser.

3. Draw a larger pyramid at Giza. This is the biggest pyramid ever constructed, the Great Pyramid of Giza.

COLORING PAGE

Pyramids *(Activity Book page 19)*

Color the architect of the first pyramids, Imhotep, as he ponders how he will build these great structures.

CRAFT PROJECT 1: PAPYRUS SCROLL

DJOSER'S DIRECTIONS TO BEGIN WORK ON HIS TOMB

Materials:
- ☐ Brown paper grocery bag
- ☐ 2 wooden rods or knitting needles (each 9 or 10 inches long)
- ☐ Brown watercolor paint
- ☐ Stapler
- ☐ Black permanent marker

Directions:

1. Cut down the sides of the paper bag. Then cut off the bottom of the bag to get a good sized rectangle with one side at least 8 in long.
2. Wrinkle the entire rectangle multiple times smoothing it back out between each time so that the bag gets an old parchment look.
3. Lay bag out flat and paint with brown watercolor paint. Let dry so bag has a glossy finish.
4. Have child or help child write a message from Djoser, the pharaoh, to Imhotep, the chief architect, directing him to begin work on his tomb.
5. Place wood rods at each end and fold just the end over and staple three or four times to secure.
6. Tightly roll up around the wooden rods on both sides. Your parchment is complete.
7. Enjoy!

CRAFT PROJECT 2: EGYPTIAN TOILET PAPER TUBE MUMMY

Materials:
- ☐ Toilet paper rolls
- ☐ White yarn
- ☐ Googly eyes
- ☐ Glue
- ☐ Tape

Directions:

1. Tape long piece of white yarn to the inside of the toilet paper roll. Begin wrapping upward around the outside of the roll (leaving room for the face) to look like a mummy.
2. Tape end of yarn in place.
3. Glue on googly eyes.
4. Enjoy!

DRAWING PROJECT: SARCOPHAGUS

Materials:
- ☐ Drawing paper
- ☐ Pencil
- ☐ Eraser
- ☐ Colored pencils
- ☐ Template from Activity Book *(Activity Book page 21–22)*

Directions:

1. Use the template in the Activity book to instruct your child on how to draw a sarcophagus. Use whatever scale you want for your drawing.

2. Have your child color his or her sarcophagus.

3. Enjoy!

SNACK PROJECT 1: EGYPTIAN HOT DOG MUMMY

Ingredients:
- ☐ 1-2 packages hotdogs
- ☐ 1-2 cans crescent rolls
- ☐ Mustard
- ☐ Pizza cutter

Directions:

1. Preheat oven to 375° F (or temperature suggested on dough can).

2. Lay out prepared crescent roll dough and push together any seams.

3. Using pizza cutter, cut dough into 1 inch long strips.

4. Wrap dough strips around hot dogs starting at bottom and leaving 1-2 inches at the top. Using remaining strips of dough wrap the headdress around the top of the hotdog leaving room for eyes.

5. Set on cookie sheet and place in preheated oven for 12-15 minutes or until dough is golden brown.

6. Remove and let cool for a few minutes then use mustard to add the eyes to your Egyptian mummy hotdog.

7. Enjoy!

SNACK PROJECT 2: THE GREAT PYRAMID MARSHMALLOW TREAT

Ingredients:

- ☐ 5 cups crispy rice cereal
- ☐ 4 cups of mini marshmallows
- ☐ 3 Tbsp. butter
- ☐ 1/2 tsp. vanilla

Directions:

1. Use a large saucepan to melt butter over low heat.
2. Add the vanilla.
3. Add the marshmallows and stir until completely melted.
4. Turn off the heat and add the cereal.
5. Allow to cool slightly (about 30 minutes).
6. Fashion into a pyramid shape and allow to completely cool.
7. Enjoy!

CHAPTER 4
The Land Between Two Rivers

QUESTIONS FOR REVIEW:

1. **What were Anen and his father searching for in the opening story?**

   The lapis lazuli, which was a rare stone the pharaoh wanted to place in his crown.

2. **List at least two of the things the Sumerians were the first people to do.**

   Developed writing, built sailboats, used irrigation, domesticated animals, and invented the time system.

3. **Describe what a ziggurat is.**

   It was where the Sumerian people worshiped their gods. It looked much like the Egyptian pyramids but had temples at the top that were reached by massive staircases.

4. **What was the form of writing that the Sumerians used and what did it look like?**

   It was called cuneiform and it was made of wedge-shaped marks pressed into wet clay. The word "cuneiform" literally means "wedge-shaped."

5. **Who wrote down one of the world's first law codes?**

   Hammurabi, the Babylonian king.

NARRATION EXERCISES:

The Sumerians

They were a people who lived in Sumer in southern Mesopotamia. Unlike the Egyptians who were mostly farmers and lived in villages, the Sumerians mostly lived in cities. They had no single ruler or king, but rather had leaders who governed each city, or "city-state." They invented many important things, including the use of writing (called cuneiform), building sailboats, the use of irrigation, the domestication of animals, and the invention of the time system. They also constructed ziggurats which was where they worshipped their gods. These were much like Egyptian pyramids but had temples at the top reached by massive staircases. The Sumerians were busy people; they were builders, laborers, wood workers, potters, coppersmiths, weavers, sculptors, fishermen, gardeners, and merchants.

Gilgamesh

The Epic of Gilgamesh is a Sumerian story about a man searching for the secret to eternal life after the death of his friend. He travels far and wide in search of something that will help him defeat death. He eventually finds a plant that will do so. But on his way home he loses the plant when a snake eats it. Though he is saddened by what he lost, he learns a valuable lesson—death comes to us all and the best we can do is cherish the life we have.

Activity Projects

MAP ACTIVITY: THE LAND BETWEEN TWO RIVERS
(Activity Book page 23)

1. Locate the Tigris and the Euphrates Rivers and trace both in blue.
2. Locate the city of Memphis on the map and circle it in green.
3. Locate the region of Sumer on the map and draw a large circle in green over the region.
4. Use a darker blue to trace a path between Memphis and Sumer—this would be the path of Merniptah from our story in the chapter.
5. Color the land between the Tigris and Euphrates yellow. This is Mesopotamia, or "land between the rivers".

COLORING PAGE

Gilgamesh *(Activity Book page 25)*

Color the picture of Gilgamesh after he discovers the plant of immortality.

CRAFT PROJECT 1: MAKE A LAPIS LAZULI STONE

Materials:
- ☐ Smooth stones
- ☐ Old toothbrush
- ☐ Blue paint
- ☐ Water sealer or clear nail polish
- ☐ Small paint brush

Directions:

1. Use the old toothbrush to scrub your rock(s) clean under running water.

2. Allow rock to dry completely.

3. Paint your rock blue and allow it to dry again.

4. Use the paint brush and apply the water sealer. Several coats work best to give it the optimum shine.

5. Enjoy!

CRAFT PROJECT 2: SUMERIAN CLOCK

Materials:
- ☐ Paper plate
- ☐ Mini metal bracket or paper fastener
- ☐ Construction paper (color of your choice)
- ☐ Markers (color of your choice)

Directions:

1. Using a marker and the paper plate, write the numbers 1-12 for the clock face.

3. Draw and cut out an hour and minute hand for your clock from the colored construction paper.

4. Attach the hour and minute hands to the center of the clock face with the metal bracket.

5. Remind your child that the Sumerians invented the time system based on sixty second minutes and sixty minute hours that we still use today.

6. Enjoy!

CRAFT PROJECT 3: PAPER PLATE SNAKE WIND TWIRLER WHO ATE GILGAMESH'S PLANT OF IMMORTALITY

Materials:

- ☐ Paper plate
- ☐ Green, brown, black, any color washable paint for your snake
- ☐ Hot glue gun
- ☐ Red yarn
- ☐ Googly eyes
- ☐ Scissors

Directions:

1. Paint both sides of your paper plate any color you want the body of your snake to be.
2. Use a pencil to draw in a spiral beginning at the outside of the plate and circling your way inward (rings should be 1 to 1 1/2 inch thick).
3. Hot glue on googly eyes at the center circle of the paper plate.
4. Use scissors to cut along the circular lines being sure to leave a small circular area in the middle of your plate.
5. Use the hot glue gun to adhere the red yarn to your plate.
6. Holding the yarn run with your snake behind you and watch as it twirls in the wind.
7. Enjoy!

CHAPTER 5
Egyptian Empires

QUESTIONS FOR REVIEW:

1. **What were the paths called that allowed for trading between Egypt and Mesopotamia?**

   Trade routes.

2. **What was it about the Hyksos that overwhelmed the Egyptians in their warfare with them?**

   They rode and fought on horseback.

3. **What strange thing did the female pharaoh, Hatshepsut, do to make herself look more like a man?**

   Hatshepsut wore a fake beard.

4. **What is tribute?**

   Money paid from one people or kingdom to another as a sign of submission.

5. **Who was the warrior pharaoh who reigned for 54 years and never lost a battle?**

   Thutmose.

NARRATION EXERCISES:

Chariots

   These were small carts pulled by a team of horses and were used in battle by the Egyptians. Two men would often stand in them, one navigating the horses and holding a shield to protect them, while the other shot arrows at the enemy.

Rameses II

Ramses II rose to the Egyptian throne in 1279 B.C. and was inspired by the glory of Egypt's past conquests. He wanted to recover the empire of Thutmose and had the leadership and intelligence to do so. He moved the capital of Egypt to the north, to a city called Pi-Rameses. This was closer to Canaan, making it easier for Egyptian armies to go and return from war. He attacked the cities of Canaan and Syria, winning great victories and bringing home much tribute. Rameses fought the largest chariot battle in history over a city called Kadesh, located in Syria. He left behind many statues and monuments, many of which still survive to this day.

Activity Projects

MAP ACTIVITY: TRADE BETWEEN MESOPOTAMIA AND EGYPT (*Activity Book page 27*)

1. Color Egypt lightly in red.
2. Color Mesopotamia lightly in green.
3. Use brown to draw a route between the two which passes through Canaan. Canaan became a very important territory because it was positioned right along the trade route between Egypt and Mesopotamia.

COLORING PAGE

Rameses on his Chariot (*Activity Book page 29*)

Color the picture of Ramses as he fires arrows from his chariot at the Battle of Kadesh.

CRAFT PROJECT 1: HYKSOS CLOTHES PIN HORSE

Materials:

- ☐ 2 wooden clothes pins
- ☐ Brown paint
- ☐ Markers
- ☐ Yarn (brown, black, or tan)
- ☐ Template from Activity Book (*Activity Book page 31*)
- ☐ Scissors
- ☐ Glue

Directions:

1. Color your template from the activity book and cut out the pieces for your horse.
2. Paint the clothes pins brown and let dry.
3. Glue the two sides of the horse template together.
4. Attach the dried clothes pins to the bottom of your horse's body for its legs.
5. Use a few pieces of yarn to create a mane and a tail to glue to both sides of your horse.
6. Enjoy!

DRAWING PROJECT: HOW TO DRAW A HORSE

Materials:
- ☐ Drawing paper
- ☐ Pencil
- ☐ Eraser
- ☐ Colored pencils
- ☐ Template from Activity Book *(Activity Book page 33–35)*

Directions:

1. Use the template in the Activity book to instruct your child on how to draw a horse. Use whatever scale you want for your drawing.
2. Have your child color his or her horse.
3. Enjoy!

CHAPTER 6
Peoples of the Levant

QUESTIONS FOR REVIEW:

1. **What was the strip of land at the far eastern end of the Mediterranean Sea connecting Egypt and Mesopotamia?**

   The Levant.

2. **How did the Egyptians and Hittites make peace?**

   Through the marriage of Rameses and King Hattusilis's daughter, Princess Bentresh.

3. **What is a vizier?**

   A chief servant, or the head of pharaoh's household.

4. **What were hilltop cities of the Canaanite people called?**

   A "tell."

5. **Why was the Phoenician alphabet so much easier to learn than the Egyptian hieroglyphics?**

   Because it was alphabetic, meaning each symbol represented a sound, as opposed to pictographic, where each word is represented by a picture. It was far easier to remember 26 letters than over 3,000 picture-symbols.

NARRATION EXERCISES:

The Hittites

They were a rugged, mountain-dwelling folk who settled in the highlands of Anatolia around 2000 B.C. Hittite cities were far up in the highlands of Anatolia, sometimes right in the mountains. This gave them protection from their enemies and these highlands were good for horse grazing. The Hittites grew powerful and conquered many lands, including taking over various trade routes which brought them wealth. Only when they ran into the Egyptians were they defeated. The Hittites left behind very little for us to learn from them.

The Phoenicians

The Phoenicians dwelt in the cities of Tyre and Sidon on the coast of the Mediterranean and were known as sea people. From their twin cities they sent ships throughout the Mediterranean, trading and spreading their culture. They were a wealthy people with great riches, but the greatest gift of Phoenicia was her alphabet. Their writing was alphabetic, meaning each symbols represented a sound. Compared to the pictographic hieroglyphics of Egypt and the cuneiform of Mesopotamia, this was much easier to learn and remember. Our own English writing comes from ancient Phoenician.

Activity Projects

MAP ACTIVITY: THE LEVANT *(Activity Book page 37)*

1. Locate the area labeled "Hittites" and shade it orange.
2. Locate the area labeled "Canaan" and shade it green.
3. Locate the cities of Tyre and Sidon, circle them in blue, and write over them "Phoenicians."

CROSSWORD PUZZLE: PEOPLES OF THE LEVANT
(Activity Book page 39)

Across:
- 4. Canaan
- 6. Phoenicians
- 8. Egypt

Down:
- 1. Anatolia
- 2. Sheep
- 3. Levant
- 4. Cedar
- 5. Alphabet
- 7. Hittites

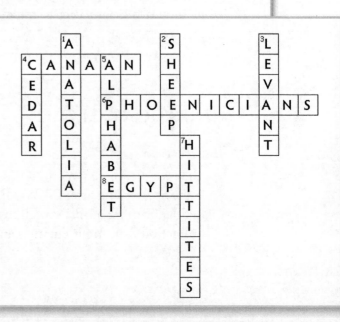

SNACK PROJECT: CANAANITE FIG BARS

Ingredients:

Crust and topping:
- ☐ 3/4 cup butter, softened
- ☐ 1 cup packed brown sugar
- ☐ 1 1/2 cups all-purpose flour
- ☐ 1 tsp. salt
- ☐ 1/2 tsp. baking soda
- ☐ 1 1/4 cups quick-cooking oats

Filling:
- ☐ 1/4 cup granulated sugar
- ☐ 1 cup boiling water
- ☐ 9 oz dried figs, chopped
- ☐ 1/2 cup apple butter

Directions:
1. Preheat oven to 350.
2. Beat butter and sugar until fluffy.
3. Mix flour, salt, baking soda, and oats and stir into butter mixture.
4. Press a little over half into the bottom of a 9 x 13 pan sprayed with cooking spray.
5. Cook sugar, water and figs over medium high heat until most of the liquid is absorbed / cooked off.
6. Remove from heat and stir in apple butter.
7. Spread fig mixture over cookie bar base.
8. Crumble remaining flour / oat mixture and sprinkle as topping for cookie bar.
9. Bake 20-25 minutes. Watch closely.
10. Enjoy!

CHAPTER 7
The God of Israel

QUESTIONS FOR REVIEW:

1. **What is the first book of the Bible in which we can read about the story of Abraham?**
   The Book of Genesis.

2. **What was the great sadness that Abraham and Sarah had in their lives?**
   They could not have any children.

3. **What is it called when there is not enough food for the people to eat?**
   A famine.

4. **How did Moses' mother save him from the being killed by the Egyptians?**
   She placed him in a basket made of reeds and pushed him down the river, where he was taken in by an Egyptian princess.

5. **What body of water did Moses part with his staff?**
   The Red Sea.

NARRATION EXERCISES:

Abraham

His story is preserved for us in the Book of Genesis, the first book of the Bible. He lived in the Sumerian city of Ur around 1800 B.C. and was a member of the tribe known as the Hebrews. He was a wealthy merchant and had many servants and flocks, but he and his wife, Sarah, were not able to have children, which made them both very sad. But God one day revealed Himself to Abraham and promised him a son, and that he would become a father of a great nation. God asked Abraham to move to the land of Canaan, and so he did. Abraham and his wife did eventually have a son, named Isaac, and a great line of descendants would follow.

Moses

He was born during a time when the Egyptians were persecuting the Israelites. To keep him from being murdered, his mother sent him down the river in a basket. An Egyptian princess found him and took him into her home, where he was raised. But later he learned of his true heritage and his mission to set the Israelite people free. God spoke to him and had him lead his people out of Egypt. As the Egyptians pursued them, Moses parted the Red Sea with his staff and saved his people. Later, he would be given the Ten Commandments by God, which were rules and laws for how to live a just life and follow God's will.

Activity Projects

MAP ACTIVITY 1: GOD CALLS ABRAHAM *(Activity Book page 41)*

1. Locate Ur on the map and circle it with blue. This is the city where Abram lived with his wife and father. Draw a line from Ur up through Haran and then down to the land of Canaan.

2. Circle Canaan and shade the entire area blue. This is the land God told Abraham he would give to his descendants.

MAP ACTIVITY 2: ISRAELITES' EXODUS FROM EGYPT
(Activity Book page 43)

1. Trace a path in brown from the Land of Goshen to Mount Horeb / Mount Sinai.

2. Where the route crosses the Red Sea, draw Moses' staff to show that this is where God worked the miracle of parting the Red Sea.

3. At the area labeled Mount Sinai, draw a tablet indicating this is where Moses received the Ten Commandments.

CRAFT PROJECT 1: MOSES BASKET ON THE NILE

Materials:

- ☐ Paper plate
- ☐ White muffin liner
- ☐ Green construction paper
- ☐ Modeling clay
- ☐ Blue and brown markers
- ☐ Stapler

Directions:

1. Color the paper plate blue (this will be our Nile River). You can add fish to the water if desired.
2. Color the muffin liner brown (this will be our basket for Moses) and glue in the center of the plate.
3. Cut an 8" x 3" section of green construction paper and staple along the edge of the plate (positioning does not matter).
4. Cut vertical slits in the green construction paper (these are our reeds along the banks of the Nile).
5. Mold a baby from the clay and allow to dry and harden. Use markers to create a face and blanket for baby Moses.
6. Place Moses in the middle of his basket.
7. Enjoy!

CRAFT PROJECT 2: BURNING BUSH

Materials:
- ☐ Blue, green, and brown construction paper
- ☐ Brown and green markers
- ☐ Red, yellow, and orange tissue paper
- ☐ Glue

Directions:

1. Cut a strip of green construction paper to be the ground and glue it to the bottom blue construction paper (which is the sky).
2. Use a brown marker to draw a bush and branches.
3. Use the green marker to add leaves to the bush.
4. Cut flame-like strips from the various colors of tissue paper and glue them onto the bush.
5. Enjoy!

DRAWING PROJECT: MOSES PARTING THE RED SEA

Materials:
- ☐ Template from Activity Book *(Activity Book page 44–46)*
- ☐ Drawing paper
- ☐ Pencil
- ☐ Colored pencils

Directions:

1. Instruct your child on how to draw Moses according to the steps on the template.
2. Color Moses with the sea parting behind him.
3. Enjoy!

SNACK PROJECT: HOT MILK AND HONEY DRINK

Ingredients:

- ☐ 2 cups milk
- ☐ 2 tsp. honey
- ☐ 1/2 tsp vanilla
- ☐ Pinch of cinnamon, if desired

Directions:

1. Place ingredients in saucepan and warm over medium heat, stir to prevent burning.
2. Pour into mugs.
3. Enjoy!

CHAPTER 8
The Kingdom of David

QUESTIONS FOR REVIEW:

1. **Who was Moses' assistant who led the Israelites after Moses died?**
   Joshua.

2. **What was the Ark of the Covenant?**
   The special golden box which housed the Ten Commandments.

3. **What was Solomon most known for?**
   His wisdom, and that he built the Temple in Jerusalem.

4. **Who were the people inspired to speak on God's behalf?**
   Prophets.

5. **Where were the inhabitants of the Kingdom of Judea taken captive?**
   Babylon.

NARRATION EXERCISE:

Joshua's Conquest of Jericho

Joshua took over after the death of Moses in leading the Israelite people. He led them into Canaan where they fought many battles. One famous battle was the sacking of Jericho. God instructed Joshua and the Israelites to walk around the city for seven days carrying the Ark of the Covenant. On the seventh day they were to walk around seven more times, and then the priests were to blow their trumpets and the men were to scream. They had faith in God and did what He asked. Once they did, the walls of the mighty city of Jericho fell and they were able to take the city.

The Prophets

These were holy men who spoke on God's behalf to all the people. Most of the famous prophets came after the kingdom of David split and the people began to fall away from God. They preached that the Israelites should stop committing evil deeds and obey God's law sincerely, and that it was much more important to serve God with a pure heart than to offer sacrifices. The prophets were not always well-liked and some kings had them persecuted. But the prophets taught that one day God would send a special ruler called a Messiah who was a kind of priest-king. The prophets said he would turn the hearts of the people back to God and establish a kingdom of justice. He would write the law of God in peoples' hearts so they would be able to serve Him faithfully.

Activity Projects

MAP ACTIVITY: JOSHUA, DAVID, AND SOLOMON
(Activity Book page 47)

1. Locate Jericho on your map and with brown, draw walls around it showing the fortifications that were in place when Joshua reached the city.

2. Draw a trumpet beside Jericho showing that Joshua obeyed God and marched around the city every day for seven days, and then on the seventh day marched around the city seven times and ordered the priests to blow their trumpets and every man to shout.

3. Locate Jerusalem on the map and in blue write above it "City of David" which is what King David called the city when he conquered it.

4. Using purple, draw a temple beside Jerusalem and label it "temple for God." This is the temple constructed by King Solomon.

COLORING PAGE

Jericho and the Ark *(Activity Book page 49)*

Color the picture of Joshua and the Israelites carrying the Ark around the walls of Jericho.

CRAFT PROJECT 1: TOILET PAPER / PAPER TOWEL ROLL DAVID AND GOLIATH

Materials:
- ☐ Template from Activity Book *(Activity Book page 51–53)*
- ☐ Colored pencils
- ☐ Craft glue
- ☐ Scissors

Directions:
1. Remove the template from the Activity Book and color the David and Goliath figures.
2. Cut to the size of the toilet paper and paper towel rolls.
3. Use craft glue to attach David and Goliath to the rolls.
4. Enjoy!

CRAFT PROJECT 2: TRUMPET AT JERICHO

Materials:
- ☐ Paper towel roll
- ☐ Markers
- ☐ Scissors
- ☐ 4 buttons
- ☐ Hot glue gun

Directions:
1. Color the paper towel roll any colors you would like your trumpet to be.
2. Cut 5, 3 inch slits along one end of the paper towel roll, and bend slits out slightly.
3. Glue the 4 buttons into place to be the trumpet keys.
4. Enjoy!

SNACK PROJECT: GRAHAM CRACKER JERICHO

Ingredients:
- ☐ Sandwich bread
- ☐ Graham crackers
- ☐ Peanut butter or almond butter
- ☐ Gummy bears

Directions:

1. Make a peanut butter or almond butter sandwich. Coat the outside crust with more peanut or almond butter.

2. Break your graham crackers along lines.

3. Line up each graham cracker piece vertically along the outside of the sandwich (this is our wall around Jericho so the graham cracker should be taller than the sandwich - the peanut or almond butter is our bonding agent to keep the graham crackers from falling).

4. March the gummy bears around the outside wall.

5. On the final lap every one gives a shout and you knock down the graham cracker wall.

6. Enjoy!

CHAPTER 9
The Bearded Kings of the North

QUESTIONS FOR REVIEW:

1. **What battle skill did the Assyrians master that made them so fierce?**

   They learned to ride on horses, even to the point where they could ride and shoot bows at the same time.

2. **Describe the Assyrian battering ram.**

   It was a great log with a pointed tip of iron. They would tie it to long ropes and swing it back and forth, and rest it on wheeled carts, so that they could smash it into the walls of the cities they invaded.

3. **What does it mean when we say the Assyrians practiced deportation of the people they conquered?**

   It means they gathered them up and forced them leave their homes to go live somewhere else.

4. **What is a man-made tunnel or channel that carries water into the city?**

   An aqueduct.

5. **Why did people dislike the Assyrians and eventually revolt against them?**

   They were very cruel to the people they conquered.

NARRATION EXERCISES:

Reliefs

These were a famous kind of Assyrian sculpture. The figures were carved so they are higher than the surrounding material. They had a three dimensional look. Assyrian reliefs showed that the men were tall and muscular, with long, heavy beards. The Assyrian kings wore the biggest beards of all, sometimes down to their chest. The beards were often curled and adorned with gold ringlets.

Nineveh

The capital of Assyria located along the banks of the Tigris River. This city was made great by one of Assyria's most powerful kings, Sennacherib. He constructed a gigantic palace in the center of the city, and built sprawling gardens with artificial rivers. The streets were widened and he raised great temples to the gods of Assyria. The city walls were also strengthened. Under Sennacherib, Nineveh became the greatest city in the world and home to over 300,000 people.

Activity Projects

MAP ACTIVITY: ASSYRIAN EMPIRE *(Activity Book page 55)*

1. Locate Assyria on the map. Draw a bow and arrow beside Assyria indicating that they came to power because they mastered the horse and learned to shoot an arrow while riding.

2. Draw a red star at Nineveh indicating that this was the capital city of Assyria.

CRAFT PROJECT 2: MAKE A SEA COW

Materials:
- ☐ Light grey modeling clay
- ☐ Markers

Directions:

1. Do an encyclopedia or internet search to get a good idea of what a hippopotamus looks like.

2. Use modeling clay to form your sea cow (now know as the hippopotamus).

3. Follow clay instructions to allow your model to harden.

4. Use markers to color eyes, mouth, and any other parts you desire.

5. Enjoy!

CRAFT PROJECT 3: AQUEDUCT

Materials:
- ☐ Plastic straws
- ☐ Duct tape
- ☐ Small paper cups (bathroom cups)
- ☐ Objects from around the house to create slope for aqueduct
- ☐ Bowl

Directions:

1. Cut a hole in the side (near the bottom) of a bathroom cup just big enough to fit one end of your straw through. Slide straw into hole and duct tape around hole to prevent water leakage.
2. Attach straw end to end and duct tape at these joints. Create angles to your aqueduct by placing more bathroom cups along your route.
3. Stack your starting cup high and support your straws along your route.
4. End your aqueduct in a bowl to collect the water.
5. Pour water into the starting cup and watch the water travel through your aqueduct and out the other end into your bowl.
6. Enjoy!

CHAPTER 10
The Splendor of Babylon

QUESTIONS FOR REVIEW:

1. **What was a vassal?**

   The lands and cultures that Babylon ruled over by receiving tribute and allegiance from them.

2. **How did Babylon treat their vassals?**

   They treated them with respect because they did not want to rule through fear. They allowed their subjects to be educated and trained.

3. **While King Nabopolassar specialized in running the government, what did his son, Nebuchadnezzar, specialize in?**

   Warfare. He was an excellent commander and popular with his men.

4. **Who was the Judean King who rebelled against Nebuchadnezzar?**

   Zedekiah

5. **What led to the fall of Babylon?**

   King Nebuchadnezzar died, leaving his sons to war with one another and plot to kill each other. The division weakened the kingdom and they were eventually conquered by the Persians.

NARRATION EXERCISES:

King Nebuchadnezzar

He was the son of the Babylonian King Nabopolassar. Nebuchadnezzar became king at the young age of 29, enjoying a long reign of forty-three years. He was the most successful of all the rulers of Babylon. He defeated many other armies, including over the Egyptians and the Kingdom of Judea. After marching on Jerusalem, he took thousands of young Judeans captive and sent them to Babylon to be educated as Babylonians. But at times, Nebuchadnezzar preferred to make peace treaties rather than wage war. He married Princess Amytis of the Medes to unite the two kingdoms. He eventually created the famous Hanging Gardens to please his queen and lessen her homesickness. Besides the Hanging Gardens, Nebuchadnezzar also oversaw the construction of great walls around the city of Babylon, and the reconstruction of great ziggurats. Under Nebuchadnezzar, Babylon became a magnificently prosperous city, but it would collapse shortly after his death as his sons warred with one another and were eventually conquered by the Persians.

Hanging Gardens

These were constructed in Babylon by King Nebuchadnezzar as a gift to his Median queen, Amytis. She missed the lush mountains of her homeland after she was forced to move to Babylon, so he brought the mountains to her. The Hanging Gardens were a type of terraced pyramid built within the city. They were estimated at three stories high, maybe more, and each terrace contained a garden filled with exotic plants imported from Media. Some historians said that special screws were used to move water up the terraces to keep the garden watered; others said there were tubes that would spray mist at certain times. No matter what was determined about them, they were later called one of the wonders of the world.

Activity Projects

MAP ACTIVITY: THE SPLENDOR OF BABYLON
(Activity Book page 56)

1. Locate the city of Babylon. Draw a book beside Babylon to show that Nabopolassar thought that education was of the highest importance.

2. Locate city of Jerusalem which was the capital of the kingdom of Judah. With red, draw a line from Jerusalem to the city of Babylon to show that Nebuchadnezzar conquered King Zedekiah and took thousands of youth from Judah to Babylon to be educated as Babylonians.

3. Draw a flower beside Babylon to mark the wonder of the Hanging Gardens of Babylon.

COLORING PAGE

Hanging Gardens *(Activity Book page 57)*
Color the picture of King Nebuchadnezzar showing his queen the Hanging Gardens of Babylon.

WORD SEARCH: THE SPLENDOR OF BABYLON

(Activity Book page 59–60) Fill in the blanks for The Splendor of Babylon word search clues and then find the corresponding words in the word search. Note: There is a word bank at the end of the word search to aid the student.

Answer Key:

1. Nabopolassar
2. vassals
3. Babylon
4. Assyria
5. Nebuchadnezzar
6. Levant
7. Judah
8. Zedekiah
9. Amytis
10. Gardens
11. wonders
12. chariots
13. lions
14. ziggurats
15. Euphrates
16. Belshazzar

CRAFT PROJECT 1: CONSTRUCT A ZIGGURAT

Materials:
- ☐ Empty boxes various sizes, (cereal, pasta, granola bar … etc), at least 4
- ☐ Yellow or tan construction paper
- ☐ Tape
- ☐ Glue
- ☐ Markers

Directions:

1. Cover various boxes with paper grocery bags (inside out so that no print is showing).
2. Tape in place.
3. Stack at least 4 boxes one on top of another and glue together (biggest to smallest).
4. Using markers, decorate the outside of your ziggurat as desired.
5. Enjoy!

CRAFT PROJECT 2: GATES OF BABYLON

Materials:
- ☐ Large cardboard shipping box
- ☐ Blue, yellow, and orange paint
- ☐ 2 paper plates
- ☐ Brown, orange yarn
- ☐ Markers
- ☐ Super glue

Directions

1. Remove the smaller flaps on the top of the cardboard box.
2. The other two flaps will be the gates of Babylon.
3. Paint the gates blue and allow to dry.
4. In the meantime, paint the centers of both paper plates yellow and paint the outer rim orange and allow to dry (these will be lion's head and mane).
5. Cut 1/2 in thick slits all along the outer orange rim so that the mane looks more like strands.
6. Use markers to create eyes, nose and mouth for the lion.
7. Glue the lion's head to the blue gates.
8. Enjoy!

CHAPTER 11
The Rise of Persia

QUESTIONS FOR REVIEW:

1. **Who was the prophet given a vision by God of wild animals attacking each other, which represented the ancient kingdoms all warring with one another?**
   Daniel.

2. **What was the unique story about how King Cyrus came to power?**
   His grandfather, King Astyages, had a dream of Cyrus stealing his throne from him, so he tried to have him killed. But a kind-hearted servant helped him escape. When Cyrus grew older, he returned and ended up defeating his grandfather in battle and taking the throne.

3. **What was King Darius' Royal Road?**
   It was a grand road running from his capitals to the furthest boundaries of the empire. It enabled messengers to move quickly throughout the empire, and so it was a kind of primitive postal service.

4. **Darius divided his empire into smaller territories which were ruled by governors, what were these territories and governors called?**
   Satrapies (territories) and Satraps (governors).

5. **Besides being fierce warriors, what else were the Persians good at?**
   They were also great artists and sculptors.

NARRATION EXERCISES:

The Vanishing Army
   This was a group of 50,000 men sent by King Cambyses of the Persians (son of King Cyrus) into the Egyptian dessert to find an oasis called Siwa. At this oasis there was a temple to the Egyptian god Amun.

Cambyses had heard this temple was rich with treasure, so he wanted to attack and plunder it. He sent 50,000 Persian soldiers to march across the desert to attack Siwa. But the men did not return and were never seen again. People have wondered if a giant sandstorm drown them in sand, or if the Egyptians killed and buried them. There was barely any trace that they ever entered the desert. Their story remains one of the biggest mysteries of the ancient world.

The Immortals

The Persian army was considered one of the strongest of the ancient world, with possibly as many as 500,000 men. The soldiers who were the strongest and toughest were selected to serve as the king's special guards. These men, known as "Immortals," were a group of 10,000 of the best soldiers chosen to guard the Persian king in battle. It was considered a great honor for a soldier to be chosen to serve with the Immortals.

Activity Projects

MAP ACTIVITY: THE PERSIAN EMPIRE UNDER CYRUS
(Activity Book page 61)

1. Locate Babylon on the map and write "King Cyrus" beside it and draw a shepherd's crook showing that King Cyrus was referred to as a shepherd to his people.

2. Draw a line with green from Babylon to Jerusalem showing that King Cyrus allowed the Jews to return to their homeland, making the trek across the hot desert from Babylon to Jerusalem.

COLORING PAGE

King Cyrus *(Activity Book page 63)*
Color the picture of King Cyrus, ruler of the Persians.

VANISHING ARMY MAZE

(Activity Book page 65) Can you help King Cambyses' army make it to Siwa? This is a very difficult maze, it could be that your army, like that of King Cambyses, will disappear en route.

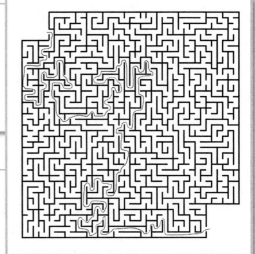

ACTIVITY PROJECT: VANISHING ARMY TRICK

Materials:
- ☐ 3 pieces of paper, two the same color
- ☐ Ruler
- ☐ Pencil
- ☐ Scissors
- ☐ Glue stick
- ☐ Scotch tape
- ☐ Army template in Activity Book *(Activity Book page 67)*
- ☐ A glass

Directions:
1. Place the top of the glass on one of the sheets of construction paper that you have 2 of, and trace it around the rim.
2. Cut out the circle you traced.
3. Put craft glue around the glass and place your circle on the glue, over the rim.
4. Take the other color construction paper and cut a rectangle that will completely wrap around your glass as a paper tube.
5. Tape the wrapped rectangle around your glass.
6. Use the second piece of construction paper that is the same color as your glass top piece as a mat to do the trick on.
7. Cut out your army.
8. Let your audience know that you are going to make the army disappear.
9. Place the army paper on the mat beside the glass.
10. Put your paper tube over the glass.
11. Lift the glass and tube together and place them over the army.
12. Lift the tube off of the glass and …. ta da! the army is gone.
13. Enjoy!

CRAFT PROJECT: MAKE A PERSIAN RELIEF SCULPTURE

Materials:

- ☐ Bar of unused soap
- ☐ Soap carving pattern template in Activity Book *(Activity Book page 69)*
- ☐ Carving tools (these can be as simple as fork, plastic knives, and toothpicks or can be true tools if you have them)

Directions:

1. Gather your tools for carving.

2. Looking at your template of choice, try to create what you want in the top of your soap bar.

3. Enjoy!

CHAPTER 12
People of the Isles

QUESTIONS FOR REVIEW:

1. **What did many cultures of the ancient world consider as the end of the world, that the Israelite prophets called, "the great unknown?"**

   The Mediterranean Sea.

2. **What sort of scenes and things did the frescoes found on Crete depict?**

   Beautiful women picking flowers, servants carrying goods, men fishing or playing sports, and others of birds, dolphins, or other wildlife.

3. **How did Sir Arthur Evans come up with the name for the Minoans?**

   He named them this after King Minos, who was a figure in popular Greek myths. King Minos was a legendary King of Crete who kept a monster called the Minotaur locked beneath his palace.

4. **Why did the Minoans not have to worry as much about being invaded by foreign peoples as the other ancient cultures did?**

   Because they lived on an island, the sea protected them from foreign threats.

5. **Who wrote the Iliad?**

   The Greek poet, Homer.

NARRATION EXERCISES:

Crete

This long, narrow island, only 160 miles from east to west, is filled with rugged mountains that stretch across the entire island, except for a few plains in the north. Within the valleys and gorges created by the mountains are lush valleys filled with cypress, pines, and other hardy trees. A few lakes and several gushing rivers provide freshwater to the island. Crete's many hills are covered in lovely wild-flowers. The British archaeologist Sir Arthur Evans discovered sprawling palaces with hundreds of rooms, great courtyards, storage buildings, broad streets, and much more. These structures were as grand as anything found in Egypt and were discovered at a place called Knossos. Evans also found frescoes which taught him about the people who lived in Knossos, known as the Minoans. Frescoes are paintings done on the plaster of walls or ceilings. Most of the paintings depicted everyday scenes like beautiful women picking flowers, servants carrying goods, and men fishing or playing sports. Some frescoes were of birds, dolphins, or other wildlife.

Minoans

These people lived on Crete and took their name from the ancient Greek myths about King Minos. Sir Arthur Evans thought they lived between 1700-1500 B.C. There is great debate about where the Minoans came from, but it remains mostly a mystery. The Minoans seem to have been a joyful and peace-loving people. Since they lived on an island, they did not need to worry about being invaded by foreign armies. They spent their days farming the rich fields of northern Crete and fishing in the Mediterranean. The Minoans also valued sports highly. Many of their frescoes depict sporting events, especially the bull leaping game. The cities of the Minoans appeared to have all been destroyed around 1450 B.C. There was no evidence of violence. Most archaeologists think a massive earthquake struck the island and threw down the Minoan cities.

Activity Projects

MAP ACTIVITY: CRETE AND THE MINOAN PEOPLE
(Activity Book page 71)

1. Locate the island of Crete and draw a tree and flower here indicating the lush landscape.
2. Locate Knossos and write "Minoan People" above it, showing that the Minoan people built Knossos.
3. Circle Mycenae with red and draw a line from Mycenae to Crete showing that the Mycenaeans sailed to Crete and other islands in the eastern Mediterranean bringing these lands under their control.

COLORING PAGE

Minoan Bull Leaping Games *(Activity Book page 73)*

Color the picture of the boy leaping over the bull in the Minoan Kingdom at Knossos.

CROSSWORD PUZZLE: PEOPLES OF THE ISLES

(Activity Book page 75)

Across:
- 3. Bull
- 4. Minoans
- 8. Minotaur
- 9. Minos
- 10. Knossos

Down:
- 1. Islands
- 2. Frescoes
- 4. Mediterranean
- 5. Evans
- 6. Homer
- 7. Crete

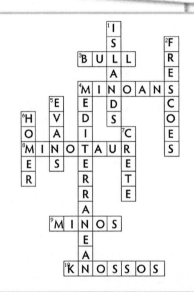

CRAFT PROJECT: CREATE A FRESCO

Materials:
- ☐ Plaster of Paris
- ☐ Plastic plate
- ☐ Paint
- ☐ Paint brushes
- ☐ Tooth picks

Directions:

1. Decide on design for fresco (either draw out your own or Google "Leaping Bull Fresco" for an idea).
2. Mix the plaster of Paris according to package directions.
3. Pour the plaster into the plastic plate.
4. When plaster begins to harden, trace an outline for your fresco.
5. Paint as desired.
6. Enjoy!

CHAPTER 13
The Founding of Greece

QUESTIONS FOR REVIEW:

1. **What is a labyrinth?**

   It is like a maze.

2. **How did Daedalus and his son, Icarus, escape from the tower where King Minos had them imprisoned?**

   Daedalus fashioned wings for himself and his son, using feathers held together with melted wax. Daedalus and Icarus were able to fly away from Crete towards Greece.

3. **What kind of land mass is Greece?**

   It is a peninsula, meaning it is surrounded by water on all its sides except one, where it is connected to the mainland.

4. **Who were some of the great warrior heroes of Mycenaean culture?**

   Achilles, Ajax, and Diomedes.

5. **What physical limitation did the Greek poet Homer suffer from?**

   He was blind.

NARRATION EXERCISES:

Greece

This mountainous peninsula sits at the bottom of Europe. Since it was such a small peninsula, the people living there were never far from the water and so loved the sea. They sailed all over the Aegean settling its many islands. Some of the peoples who lived there were the Mycenaeans and the Dorians. The Mycenaeans were fearsome in battle. All of the great heroes of the Mycenaean age were mighty warriors, men like

Achilles, Ajax, and Diomedes. The Dorians came from the north and eventually intermarried with the Mycenaeans, so that they were all just "Greeks." The Greeks loved their stories. Some of the most famous epics, the Iliad and the Odyssey, were written by the Greek poet Homer.

Trojan War

The Greek poet Homer wrote about this conflict between the Greeks and the Trojans in his epic, the *Iliad*. The Greeks attacked the city of Troy because the Greek princess, Helen, had been stolen by a Trojan prince named Paris. The battle ensued for many years, until a Greek name Odysseus came up with a clever idea. The Greek army built a gigantic wooden horse (later called a "Trojan Horse") which was hollow inside. Odysseus and his men crept inside the horse, while the rest of the Greeks went away and hid. The next morning, the Trojans saw nothing outside their city except the strange wooden horse. They were curious and brought the horse inside the city of Troy. That night, Odysseus and his Greek warriors crept from the wooden horse and opened the gates of the city. The other Greeks came out of hiding and stormed into Troy. By the time the Trojans woke up, the Greeks were everywhere! The Trojans were defeated and the Greeks took possession of the city. This story is still read about to this day.

Activity Projects

MAP ACTIVITY: TROJAN WAR *(Activity Book page 76)*

1. Use blue to color over the Aegean Sea.
2. Draw a line from Greece to Troy showing that the Greeks sailed over to Troy to take back their princess Helen.
3. With brown, draw a horse outside of Troy showing that this was how the Greeks outsmarted the Trojans and overtook the city.

COLORING PAGE

Trojan Horse *(Activity Book page 77)*

Color the picture of the famous Trojan Horse that the Greeks used as a trick to defeat the Trojans.

CRAFT PROJECT 1: DAEDALUS AND ICARUS SPOON PEOPLE

Materials:
- ☐ 2, 10-12 inch wooden spoons
- ☐ Templates from Activity Book *(Activity Book page 79–81)*
- ☐ Craft feathers
- ☐ Craft glue
- ☐ Markers
- ☐ Googly eyes
- ☐ Hot glue

Directions:
1. Color and cut out the Daedalus and Icarus bodies located in the Activity Book.
2. Hot glue the bodies onto the wooden spoons.
3. Cut out the wings found in Activity Book.
4. Use craft glue to adhere the feathers to the wings (both front and back side of the wings).
5. Hot glue the wings to the back of the wooden spoon.
6. Hot glue googly eyes to both spoons.
7. Create a nose and mouth for both Daedalus and Icarus.
8. Color hair on the top of the spoon.
9. Enjoy!

CRAFT PROJECT 2: TROJAN HORSE

Materials:
- ☐ Template from Activity Book *(Activity Book page 83–87)*
- ☐ White card stock paper
- ☐ Markers
- ☐ Glue stick
- ☐ Clear tape

Directions:
1. Color Trojan Horse template from Activity Book.
2. Glue the activity pages to card stock paper and then cut out the Trojan horse pieces.
3. Fold the base along the lines and set up.
4. Tape the two horses to either side of the base.
5. Attach the two yokes over the middle of the horse.
6. Tape the 4 wheels to the base.
7. Enjoy!

WRITING ASSIGNMENT: WRITE A RIDDLE POEM

Write a short riddle poem about the attack on Troy. Perhaps you are trying to get your audience to guess the name of the city, or perhaps the Trojan Horse, or maybe Helen is your subject. Whatever it is, use your imagination and think outside the box. You want to give clues, but don't be too direct. Have fun!

CHAPTER 14
Greek Mythology

QUESTIONS FOR REVIEW:

1. **What was the most famous and strongest of the Greek cities which the gods argued over being its protector?**

   Athens

2. **Who was the god of the sea who had a trident—a three-pronged spear—as a weapon?**

   Poseidon

3. **What is a myth?**

   A story invented to explain a truth about the world, or how something came to be. It can be legend (fiction), or a mix of legend and true history.

4. **Who was the mightiest of all the Greek gods?**

   Zeus

5. **Why were the gods called the Olympians?**

   Because they were said to live on Mount Olympus.

NARRATION EXERCISES:

The Greek gods

A poet named Hesiod wrote a book explaining how all the gods of Greece came to be. There was Zeus the Thunderer, the god of the sky, lightning, and justice. He was the king of the Greek gods and hence the most powerful. Zeus had two brothers, Poseidon, the ruler of the sea, and Hades, the ruler of the underworld. Zeus was married to his sister, Hera. Hera was the goddess of marriage and the family. Her symbol was the peacock. Other gods included the twins, Apollo (god of knowledge and light) and Artemis (goddess of hunters, virgins, and all animals), and Ares (god of war) and his wife, Aphrodite (goddess of love). These gods and others were called the Olympians because they were believed to dwell on Mount Olympus in northern Greece. These Greek gods were flawed; they told lies, stole things, and were often mean, vengeful, and unfaithful to each other. They could also be tricked and lied to by mortals and each other. All these differences made them different from the God of Israel, but the main difference was that the God who revealed Himself to Israel said He had made mankind in His image and likeness. But the Greeks imagined the gods in their own image and likeness.

Theseus

He was a prince of Athens and a Greek hero descended from the sun god Helios on his mother's side. On his father's side he was descended from Poseidon. In Theseus' day, Athens was under the control of Minos, King of Crete. Every nine years, King Minos forced the Athenians to send him seven young girls and seven young men. These youths were to be fed to the Minotaur, the bull-like monster Minos kept locked up in the labyrinth beneath his palace. This upset Prince Theseus so much he volunteered to be sent to the Minotaur in hopes of killing it. When Theseus arrived in Crete, the daughter of King Minos saw him and fell in love with him. Her name was Ariadne. She did not want Theseus to die in the labyrinth. Ariadne gave Theseus a ball of thread which he strung from the entrance to the labyrinth to where the Minotaur was. He eventually killed the beast with his bare hands and followed the thread to find his way back out. With the Minotaur dead, the Athenians no longer had to fear Minos. Theseus took Ariadne back to Athens with him and married her. Then he became King of Athens and reigned for many years.

Activity Projects

MAP ACTIVITY: ATHENS *(Activity Book page 89)*

1. Locate Athens on the map and circle it in red.
2. Draw a tree beside Athens, remembering that the Athenians chose Athena as their patroness because of the gift of the olive tree which would provide shade, food, oils, and other valuable things.
3. Draw a line in green from Athens to Crete showing the route of Theseus who traveled to Crete to kill the Minotaur and end the Athenians' fear of King Minos.

CRAFT PROJECT 1: MAKE POSEIDON'S TRIDENT

Materials:
- ☐ Wrapping paper tube
- ☐ 12 inch x 12 inch cardboard (does not have to be exact)
- ☐ Duct tape
- ☐ Aluminum foil
- ☐ Scissors
- ☐ Template in Activity Book *(Activity Book page 91)*

Directions:

1. Use the trident template as a guide to cut a trident shape from your piece of cardboard.

2. Cut a 9 inch slit in your wrapping paper tube.

3. Insert the cardboard trident into the slit side of the wrapping paper tube.

4. Twist the wrapping paper tube tightly around the cardboard trident and duct tape it into place.

5. Use aluminum foil to wrap the entire trident.

6. Enjoy!

CRAFT PROJECT 2: GREEK ACTOR'S MASK

Materials:
- ☐ Paper plate
- ☐ Yarn (color for hair and / or beard)
- ☐ Hot glue
- ☐ Flesh tone paint
- ☐ Fine tip markers
- ☐ Popsicle stick

Directions:

1. Paint your paper plate a flesh tone and allow to fully dry.

2. Hot glue on strands of yarn for hair and / or beard.

3. Draw eyes, nose, mouth, and ears with markers.

4. Hot glue popsicle stick to hold mask with.

5. Enjoy!

DRAMA PROJECT: GREEK DRAMA

Use your newly created actor's mask to act out a drama. Think of one of the stories you have learned. Which character will you be? Who can you enlist to take part in your drama? Who will you invite to watch? Spend as much or as little time as you want coming up with a creative way to portray one of the Greek tales. Enjoy!

MAZE: HELP THESEUS ESCAPE THE MINOTAUR

(Activity Book page 93) Help Theseus navigate the labyrinth to find and kill the Minotaur and then escape.

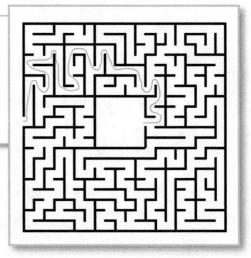

CHAPTER 15
The Cradle of Democracy

QUESTIONS FOR REVIEW:

1. **What was a polis?**

   This was the name given to individual Greek city-states, or kingdoms, all ruled by one king.

2. **What is it called when people govern themselves?**

   Democracy.

3. **What did young Spartan boys learn at their agoges?**

   That were taught to be tough, mighty warriors and to be loyal to the Spartan people.

4. **When Spartan women told their husbands going off to battle to "come back with your shield or on it," what did they mean?**

   This was a way of saying to return victorious or to not return at all, and to never surrender.

5. **What was a tyrant?**

   This was a ruler who seized control and power through force and proceeded to rule alone.

NARRATION EXERCISES:

Solon

   The Athenians turned to Solon to create fair and just laws for them. Things were very bad when he set to work. There were disagreements between different powerful families and rivalries between rich and poor. Solon ended the power of the rich over the poor by allowing all citizens—regardless of wealth—to serve in an assembly that governed the city. He abolished all debts and forbid the rich from enslaving the poor if they owed money. He also freed all slaves who were Athenians and made the voting system fairer. All of Solon's reforms made it possible for the Athenians to value education. Eventually, Solon left Athens to travel around the world for ten years. He visited other Greek cities, the islands of the Aegean, and even far away Egypt. Everywhere he went he asked the people about their laws and customs, hoping to learn as much as he could about how different people in the world lived. Solon lived to a ripe old age and died peacefully, honored by his people as a wise man.

Spartans

In the south of Greece, in a rocky peninsula known as the Peloponnesus, there was a city-state called Sparta. A great lawgiver named Lycurgus thought the most important thing for a Greek polis was to be strong, so his laws valued three things: equality, military power, and simple living. These laws led to a culture that greatly valued strength and honor. They raised their boys to be great warriors, and their girls to be proud and strong mothers. All Spartans were fiercely loyal to their people, even over loyalty to one's family. The Spartan army was the toughest and best organized in all of Greece. Like other city-states, the Spartans had assemblies that Spartan citizens voted in. But they also had two kings descended from two different royal families. These two kings, together with the Spartan assemblies, ruled the polis of Sparta.

Activity Projects

MAP ACTIVITY: ATHENS AND SPARTA *(Activity Book page 94)*

1. Locate Athens on the map and circle it in green. Write "Solon the Wise" above it showing that the people of Athens turned to Solon to create fair and just laws for them. Write "freedom and participation" beside Athens.

2. Locate Sparta on the map and circle it in blue. Write "Lycurgus" above Sparta showing that he was the great law-giver of Sparta. Write "equality, military power, and simple living" beside Sparta showing that these were the things that they valued and wanted reflected most in their laws.

COLORING PAGE:

Spartan Warrior *(Activity Book page 95)*

Color the picture of this warrior of Sparta.

WORD SEARCH: THE CRADLE OF DEMOCRACY

(Activity Book page 97–98) Fill in the blanks for The Cradle of Democracy word search clues and then find the corresponding words in the word search. Note: There is a word bank at the end of the word search to aid the student.

Answer Key:

1. Monarchy
2. polis
3. kingdom
4. democracy
5. people
6. Archons
7. Draco

8. Solon
9. laws
10. Sparta
11. agoge
12. shield
13. tyrant

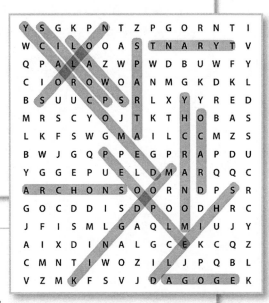

CRAFT PROJECT: SPARTAN SHIELD

Materials:

1. 12 inch diameter circular piece of cardboard (frozen pizza bottom works well)
2. 10 inch x 2 inch strip of cardboard
3. Duct tape
4. Gold paint
5. Black marker

Directions:

1. Paint your circular piece of cardboard with gold paint and let fully dry.
2. Attach the strip of cardboard to the backside of your shield using duct tape (this will be your hand hold).
3. Think of an image you often saw in Ancient Greece … perhaps a bull head, a trident, a warrior … draw it on the front of your shield or just create another design of your choice.
4. Remind the student that husbands were told to either come home with their shields or not to come home at all.
5. Enjoy!

ACTIVITY PROJECT: TAKE A POLL AND GRAPH YOUR RESULTS

Directions:

1. Instruct the child to make a list of at least 5 things that people might say that make them happy. Allow for this list to grow as the poll is conducted.

2. Poll as many people as the child can think to ask.

3. Help the child make either a bar graph or a pie graph of the results.

4. Discuss the meaning of true happiness, of how Solon viewed happiness and of how Croesus viewed happiness.

5. Enjoy!

CHAPTER 16
The Persian Wars

QUESTIONS FOR REVIEW:

1. **Who did Xerxes want to attack because they seemed to be the only culture he had not yet conquered?**

   The Greeks.

2. **What was the alliance called when the Greek kingdoms united to withstand Xerxes?**

   The Greek League.

3. **How were 300 Spartan men able to hold off Xerxes' mighty army?**

   They forced them to fight in a narrow funnel of land, which meant Xerxes' soldiers could only come at them in small numbers, evening out the fight. Since the Spartans were such fierce warriors they were able to hold their own despite being drastically outnumbered.

4. **What is a strait?**

   A very narrow waterway.

5. **How was the oracle interpreted by the Greeks that said, "Greece will be saved by walls of wood"?**

   An Athenian named Themistocles thought it meant they should battle the Persians with ships, which were made of wood.

NARRATION EXERCISES:

King Xerxes

He was the head of the Persian Empire, which at that time was the biggest and best organized empire of the ancient world. His lands stretched from Egypt all the way to Afghanistan. Its borders reached from Arabia in the south to Armenia in the north, and as far west as Asia Minor and the coast of the Aegean Sea. But Xerxes was frustrated that the Greeks were not under his control, so he took the biggest army the world had ever seen to attack them. Throughout his battles with the Greeks, he always had more men, but he suffered multiple defeats because he was outsmarted by the Greek leaders.

The Greek League

The Greek cities were very independent, but the threat posed by the Persian invasion caused them to unite. The Greek city-states knew they had to work as one if they were to resist Xerxes. They formed an alliance of all the Greek cities. The Spartans were in charge of the League's army and the Athenians of the navy. This made sense because the Spartans were such excellent warriors and the Athenians were skilled sailors. The formation of this League helped them hold off the Persian invasion.

Activity Projects

MAP ACTIVITY: KING XERXES (*Activity Book page 99*)

1. With brown, draw a bridge from Persia to Greece crossing at the Hellespont.
2. Color the land brown, showing that the army of Xerxes was so massive that it was said to turn the green land to brown desert.
3. Draw a line beginning in Persia, going over the bridge at the Hellespont around Greece and through the pass at Thermopylae.
4. Continue down to Athens where the Athenians fled in terror from Xerxes and his army. Draw flames around the city of Athens showing that Xerxes ordered the city burned.
5. Locate Salamis and draw a throne from which Xerxes watched as his grand fleet was destroyed.

COLORING PAGE

King Xerxes (*Activity Book page 101*)

Color the picture of the mighty King Xerxes of Persia who sailed to attack the Greeks.

DOUBLE PUZZLE: GREEKS VS. PERSIANS

(Activity Book page 103) Unscramble the words from the section "The Greeks vs. The Persians" Copy the letters in the numbered blocks to the blocks with the corresponding numbers at the bottom. Who won the war for the Greeks but ultimately ended up exiled because of his pride?

XESEXR	X E R X E S
RAEPIS	P E R S I A
SAIANORMI	A S I A M I N O R
GEERK ELGAUE	G R E E K L E A G U E
SATRAPN MYAR	S P A R T A N A R M Y
INHNATA VNYA	A T H E N I A N N A V Y
COKBL TEH NSU	B L O C K T H E S U N
LERMYTAPHEO	T H E R M O P Y L A E
TARSIGHT FO MASASLI	S T R A I G H T O F
	S A L A M I S

T H E M I S T O C L E S
1 2 3 4 5 6 7 8 9 10 11 12

Who won the war for the Greeks but ultimately ended up exiled because of his pride?

CRAFT PROJECT: A THRONE FOR KING XERXES

Materials:
1. Dining chair
2. Cardboard … lots and lots of cardboard … several cardboard boxes (grocery stores often have extra boxes)
3. Gold spray paint
4. Hot glue
5. Construction paper or craft jewels
6. Duct tape
7. Plastic table cloths (or another suitable covering for a large spray paint area)

Directions:
1. Neatly flatten cardboard boxes by cutting open along folds so that you are left with one large piece of cardboard. Repeat this step as necessary to attain enough cardboard.

2. You are going to be covering your chair with the cardboard pieces. Go ahead and measure lengths of cardboard to completely cover front and back sections all the way to the floor, arm rests, and seat.

3. Spray paint the cardboard pieces gold and allow to fully dry.

4. Use duct tape to secure the seams of your cardboard pieces to one another as you build your throne around your dining chair.

5. Decorate your throne with either craft jewels or with jewels you cut from construction paper.

6. A royal seat to watch your tremendous defeat.

7. Enjoy!

DRAWING PROJECT: GREEK WARSHIP

Materials:
- ☐ Drawing paper
- ☐ Pencil
- ☐ Eraser
- ☐ Colored pencils
- ☐ Template from Activity Book *(Activity Book page 104–106)*

Directions:

1. Use the template in the Activity Book to instruct your child on how to draw an ancient Greek warship. Use whatever scale you want for your drawing.

2. If desired, have your student color his or her warship.

3. Enjoy!

CHAPTER 17
Lovers of Wisdom

QUESTIONS FOR REVIEW:

1. **What is a fable?**

   A short story meant to teach a lesson.

2. **What does "philosopher" mean in Greek?**

   "Lover of wisdom."

3. **What were the Greek philosophers in the story debating?**

   What the world and everything in it was made out of.

4. **Who were the three most famous Greek philosophers?**

   Socrates, Plato, and Aristotle.

5. **How did Aristotle explain the differences between man and animals to his students?**

   He said that men have rational souls, which allows them to think and consider things.

NARRATION EXERCISES:

Philosophy

   A philosopher is someone who uses his mind to find the truth about things. The word philosopher in Greek means "lover of wisdom." The Greeks were known for having some of the first and best philosophers, who debated things like what the world was made of, what made people happy, and what a fair and just world should be like. They often gathered in public squares to debate and argue over the answers to these questions. The most well known Greek philosophers were Socrates, Plato, and Aristotle.

Aristotle

He lived from 385 to 322 B.C. and was a student of Plato. He was interested in studying the plants and animals he saw around him. Over his life, Aristotle collected hundreds of plant and animal specimens. He wrote books on how he thought their bodies worked. He also taught that man had rational souls that allowed them to think about things rationally, which separated them from the animals. Like Socrates, Aristotle also got in trouble with the Athenians. He was forced to leave Athens and continued teaching philosophy in another country.

Activity Projects

MAP ACTIVITY: GREEK PHILOSOPHY *(Activity Book page 107)*

1. Locate Athens on the map and circle it in yellow. Write Socrates, Plato, and Aristotle around the city showing that these three great philosophers taught in the city of Athens.

COLORING PAGE:

Socrates *(Activity Book page 109)*
Color the picture of the Greek philosopher, Socrates.

WRITING ASSIGNMENT: CREATE A FABLE OF YOUR OWN

1. Reflect on the story of Thales of Miletus.

2. Choose a moral for your story. For example, "What good is it to cast your eyes into the heavens if you can't even look out for what's in front of you?" Think of a moral message you would like to convey. Maybe it's about catching more flies with honey (kindness is king), or leading by example, or never giving up, or pride leading to destruction ... or anything you choose.

3. Choose a problem to be worked out. Think of Br'er Rabbit—he has to come up with a means of escape from the briar patch. Consider the Tortoise and the Hare—we quickly learn there will be a race. How about the ant and grasshopper—we see very quickly that the grasshopper is creating a dilemma for himself.

4. Now figure out which characters you will incorporate into you story and what each character will represent. For example, the rabbit in Br'er Rabbit is a trickster who succeeds by his wits. The tortoise in The Tortoise and the Hare represents our overall long-term goals.

5. Choose your setting. Will the action take place in current day, a long time ago; will it occur outdoors, at a party, under the sea?

6. Figure out how to resolve the problem you have created in a way that best conveys the moral you have chosen.

7. Make your outline and have fun working from it. Use dialogue between your characters and let them set the stage for the resolution. Be sure to highlight the moral of your story.

8. Enjoy!

CRAFT PROJECT 1: SOCRATES, PLATO, AND ARISTOTLE SPOON PEOPLE

Materials:
- ☐ 3 10-inch wooden spoons from craft store
- ☐ Templates from Activity Book *(Activity Book page 111–115)*
- ☐ Colored pencils
- ☐ Markers
- ☐ Googly eyes (if desired)
- ☐ Hot glue gun

Directions:

1. Color your Socrates, Plato, and Aristotle bodies and cut them out.

2. Hot glue the 3 bodies to the spoons.

3. Use googly eyes or markers to add your eyes.

4. Draw a mouth, nose and hair using markers.

5. Cut out the tablets for each man and trace the writings with a marker.

6. Can you figure out which tablet goes with which man?

7. Enjoy!

CRAFT PROJECT 2: CREATE YOUR OWN CHALKBOARD FOR FAMOUS ARISTOTELIAN QUOTES

Materials:
- ☐ Old picture frame
- ☐ 1/4" thick hard board cut to fit frame
- ☐ Primer
- ☐ Chalkboard paint
- ☐ Chalk
- ☐ Activity Book page of quotes *(Activity Book page 117)*

Directions:

1. Cut hard board to fit frame.

2. Spray hard board with primer.

3. Use 2-3 coats of chalkboard paint allowing each coat to dry before applying the next.

4. Use your chalk to write out famous Aristotelian quotes. See the activity book for a list of examples. Switch them up as often as you like … there are plenty to choose from.

CHAPTER 18
Greek Against Greek

QUESTIONS FOR REVIEW:

1. **What happened amongst the Greek city-states after the Persian wars?**
   They began to argue, bicker, and war amongst themselves.

2. **What was the alliance called that the Athenians formed to invade Persian territories?**
   The Delian League.

3. **What was the Parthenon?**
   A temple in Athens sitting on a hilltop dedicated to the goddess Athena. It was built during the time of Pericles.

4. **What is a terrible sickness that spreads quickly and kills many people called?**
   A plague.

5. **Who fought in the Peloponnesian War?**
   The Spartans and the Athenians.

NARRATION EXERCISES:

Pericles

He was the leader of Athens during the time of the founding of the Delian League. Pericles was a brilliant ruler who worked hard to make life better for the Athenians. He used the money of the city to help relieve the poor, and made sure the Athenian navy was strong and that Athens was beautified by lovely buildings. One of his greatest accomplishments was his construction of the temple to the goddess Athena, known as the Parthenon. It stood on the highest hilltop in Athens and had over seventy-five columns. It also had a glistening gold and ivory statue of Athena inside. As long as Pericles lived, Athens dominated Greece. But eventually disaster struck. In the year 430 B.C., a plague came to Athens. The plague killed many Athenians, including Pericles. The great age of Athenian power was coming to an end.

The Peloponnesian War

This was a war between the Spartans and the Athenians. The two sides were evenly matched. The Spartans usually won the battles on land and the Athenians usually won the battles on the sea. Thus, neither side could prevail. But then the Athenians decided to try to become allies with Syracuse, a city on an island far to the west. The Syracusans were allies with the Spartans, but the Athenians thought that if they could bring Syracuse under their control, they would be in a much better position to defeat Sparta. The Athenians sent a general named Nicias to lead an expedition to Syracuse, but it was a disaster and they were defeated. Ultimately, the Spartans won the war, but it weakened them as well. The Peloponnesian War signaled the end of Greece's power because of the destruction it brought to all Greeks.

Activity Projects

MAP ACTIVITY: ATHENIAN DOMINANCE, SPARTAN VICTORY *(Activity Book page 118)*

1. Locate the city of Delos and with yellow draw a star showing that this city served as the capital for the Delian League which was run by the Athenians.
2. Locate the city of Naxos and with red draw an "X" on the city showing that when they attempted to leave the Delian league, the Athenians came and tore down their walls.
3. Draw a blue circle around Athens and a green circle around Sparta.
4. With red draw a line from Athens to Syracuse.
5. Circle Syracuse in green showing they were allies of the Spartans.
6. Now shade Athens with green to show that they were defeated at Syracuse and the Spartans came and tore down the walls of Athens and took her wealth and territories.

SNACK PROJECT: GRAHAM CRACKER PARTHENON

Ingredients:
- ☐ Graham crackers
- ☐ Peanut butter or icing
- ☐ Pretzel twists (the thicker kind)
- ☐ Full size marshmallows
- ☐ Candies for decorating if desired

Directions:

1. Line 3 full sheets of Graham crackers side by side and cover them with peanut butter.

2. Create the inner walls of the Parthenon by setting 2 full graham cracker sheets lengthwise opposite one another and breaking a 3rd graham cracker sheet in half for the two width pieces of the inner walls. Use peanut butter along the corners to hold the graham crackers in place.

3. Now create a base for the roof by spreading peanut butter along a single graham cracker sheet and setting it atop your walls (you may find it easier to break off smaller pieces of graham crackers and lay them atop the walls).

4. Create a straight line of marshmallows down the middle of the roof base (these will support the roof).

5. Spread peanut butter along both sides of 2 sheets of graham crackers (yes, this will be messy).

6. Attach the roof by leaning the 2 sheets on the marshmallows to create a pitch for the roof. Add extra peanut butter to support the sides if needed.

7. Use peanut butter to attach the pretzel stick columns along the outside of the Parthenon.

8. Decorate with candies.

9. Enjoy!

ACTIVITY PROJECT: PELOPONNESIAN "WAR"

Play the card game "War" with the exception that one side is Sparta and other Athens. There are 2 players; one represents Sparta and the other Athens. Each player is dealt half of the deck. Simultaneously each player turns over a card and the high card wins the hand. The winning player collects his cards and places them at the bottom of his stack and the game continues. In the event that the same face value card is turned over by both players, 3 cards are placed face down while saying "I Declare War" and then a 4th card is placed face up. The highest card takes all the cards. Make sure to check out the spoils of war (the 3 face down cards from your opponent). In the event that the 4th card is also a tie, 3 more cards are placed face down and the 4th card face-up; the higher card wins. The game is won when one player has all the cards. Enjoy!

CHAPTER 19
Alexander the Great

QUESTIONS FOR REVIEW:

1. **Who was the ruler of Macedonia? He eventually became the first king of a united Greece?**

   King Philip.

2. **What famous Philosopher did Alexander study under?**

   Aristotle.

3. **Who did Alexander intend to invade just after he became king?**

   The Persians.

4. **Describe at least one shortcoming, or flaw, Alexander had.**

   At times he would drink too much and act irresponsibly. He also had a big ego and was prideful, telling his subjects to worship him like a god. Lastly, he often lost his temper.

5. **How did Alexander die?**

   He contracted a fever while in Babylon on one of his many conquests.

NARRATION EXERCISES:

Alexander the Great

He was the son of King Philip of Macedonia who united Greece under his rule. Alexander was a smart and strong boy who showed a talent for leadership from an early age. He squabbled with his father as he grew older, and was exiled for a time before returning home to take the throne after Philip's death. Alexander then went on to conquer many lands, beginning with his invasion of the Persians. He introduced the fighting alignment called the phalanx, which was when soldiers marched in a square formation with their spears sticking out on all sides. He also went on to conquer Egypt, where he founded the city named after him, Alexandria, as well as Palestine and many other lands. Though his ego and pride caused him many problems, he united many different nations under his rule which allowed for the spreading of Greek culture. He died early, at the age of thirty-three, by contracting a fever. After his death, his empire was divided up among his generals.

The Phalanx

This was a fighting formation introduced by Alexander the Great in which soldiers marched in a square with their spears sticking out toward their enemy. Some of them men held short spears that might only be eight feet. But the longer spears might be as long as twenty-five feet. When enemies fought the phalanx, it was like walking into a wall of spikes—or a giant porcupine!

Activity Projects

MAP ACTIVITY: PERSIA, GREECE, AND MACEDONIA
(Activity Book page 119)

1. Write "King Phillip" in green above Macedonia and draw two arrows headed south into Greece indicating that King Phillip overtook Greece.
2. Write "Alexander" in red beside Macedonia and draw arrows from Macedonia into Persia showing that Alexander conquered Persia.
3. Color the lands of Persia, Greece, and Macedonia all yellow indicating Alexander's dream of uniting them under one culture, the Greek culture.

COLORING PAGE

Alexander the Great *(Activity Book page 121)*

Color the picture of the great conqueror, Alexander, as he rides atop his horse and charges into battle.

CRYPTOGRAM: TO WHOM DO YOU LEAVE YOUR EMPIRE?

Code chosen at random

(Activity Book page 123) Just before Alexander the Great died, his generals and other top aides gathered around him and asked who he would leave his empire to. He smiled and gave this answer.

Answer: To the strongest

CRAFT PROJECT 1: MAKE ALEXANDER THE GREAT'S HOBBY HORSE

Materials:
- ☐ 3 foot long wooden dowel
- ☐ Poly-fil
- ☐ Men's black sock—one with a different colored toe it will work best
- ☐ Square of black felt
- ☐ Square of pink or red felt
- ☐ Square of white felt
- ☐ Fabric glue
- ☐ Knitting needle
- ☐ Brown yarn, white yarn, red yarn (Whatever color you want for mouth, nose, and mane).
- ☐ Scissors
- ☐ Two buttons (if desired)
- ☐ Hot glue gun

Directions:

1. Stuff your sock with Poly-fil and tie yarn around the opening to keep filling in place while you work.

2. Use a piece of red yarn to "sew" a mouth along the toe seam of the sock. Make a knot on the inside of one side of the mouth, pull the yarn through and across and knot on the inside of the other end.

3. Use several yarn knots to make the nose of the horse or cut out a triangular piece of felt and glue it to the sock.

4. Use either two buttons or make two eyes from the white felt with black felt in the middle and then secure eyes to either side of the horse's head. Please make note that these will come off easily and could be a choking hazard for young children!

5. Cut about 30 pieces of yarn to around 9 inches each. Pull each piece of yarn through the middle of the sock and knot the middle to create the mane. You are making the knot in the middle of the piece of yarn on the outside so that each strand of yarn creates two pieces of hair for the mane.

6. Cut out ears from the black felt and glue a small piece of pink felt to the middle to create an ear. Glue the ears to the sock on either side of the mane.

7. Insert the dowel into the sock and use hot glue along the dowel to glue the sock in place. Re-tie the yarn very tightly along the outside of the sock where it is glued.

8. Enjoy!

CRAFT PROJECT 2: SPEARS FOR ALEXANDER'S PHALANX

Materials:
- ☐ 1 empty gift wrap roll (1 roll makes 2 spears)
- ☐ Black card stock paper
- ☐ Brown duct tape

Directions:

1. Cut the tip of your spear (tear drop shape) from the black card stock.

2. Cut a 1/2 inch slit in the end of your gift wrap roll and slide the spear tip into place.

3. Use duct tape to secure your spear tip to its handle.

4. Now repeat steps 1-3 only make your second spear shorter to demonstrate the different lengths of spears used in the phalanx.

5. Enjoy!

CHAPTER 20
The Hellenistic Age

QUESTIONS FOR REVIEW:

1. **Hellenistic is another way of saying what?**

   "Greek"—it was what the Greeks called themselves ("Hellenes").

2. **What was one of the first things Alexander's generals argued over after his death?**

   Where to bury him.

3. **What did Ptolemy have built in the city of Alexandria which stood magnificently as the tallest structure in the known world at that time?**

   The Pharos Lighthouse.

4. **What is a scribe?**

   Someone trained to copy books by hand.

5. **What was Ptolemy Philadelphus' main concern for the city of Alexandria?**

   To make it a great city of learning, and so he founded a grand library there which contained all the greatest writings from around the world.

NARRATION EXERCISES:

Ptolemy

He was one of the generals of Alexander who took over part of his kingdom after the great conqueror died. Ptolemy was given charge of Egypt and took very well to the culture there, even though he was Macedonian by birth. He wanted the Egyptian people to accept him, so he dressed like an Egyptian in public and wore the double-crown of Upper and Lower Egypt. He even called himself pharaoh and worshipped the gods of the Egyptians to show the people he honored their customs.

Of the things he is most well known for are stealing the body of Alexander from another general so that he could bury his former leader in Alexandria, as well as overseeing the construction of the famous Pharos Lighthouse. Ptolemy was succeeded after his death by his son, Ptolemy Philadelphus.

The Septuagint

Literally translated as "the seventy," this references the story of the seventy Jewish scribes translating the writings of Moses for King Ptolemy Philadelphus. He locked all of them in separate cells and had them translate the writings. When he brought all the translations together, he found that they all matched exactly. This remarkable feat was considered a divine miracle. The Septuagint would end up being the Old Testament Bible the Jews used, and was even referenced by Jesus Himself.

Activity Projects

MAP ACTIVITY: AFTER ALEXANDER *(Activity Book page 124)*

1. Locate Egypt and write "Ptolemy" above it showing that he took control of Egypt after Alexander's death.
2. Using a red pencil, begin tracing a route from Babylon to Macedonia, but stop midway and draw a line straight down to Alexandria showing that Ptolemy had the body of Alexander hijacked and taken to Alexandria for burial. Draw a small coffin by Alexandria showing this is where Alexander's body was buried.
3. Draw a lighthouse at Alexandria to represent the Pharos Lighthouse.
4. Draw a book at Alexandria indicating that Ptolemy Philadelphus had a magnificent library built for the city.
5. Now write "70" inside the book showing that 70 scribes all translated the writings of Moses and other prophets from Hebrew to Greek and that all translations were identical.

COLORING PAGES:

The Story of Septuagint *(Activity Book page 125)*

Color the picture of Eleazar as he translates the writings of Moses for King Ptolemy Philadelphus.

MAZE: PTOLEMY PHILADELPHUS AND HIS LIBRARY *(Activity Book page 127)*

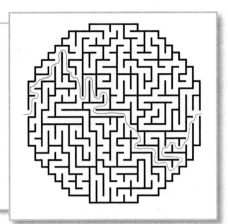

Men and women came from all over the world to study at Ptolemy's wonderful library. The journey, for many, would have been long and even dangerous, yet it was worth their effort. Can you journey through the maze to make it to Ptolemy's library?

DOUBLE PUZZLE: THE STORY OF THE SEPTUAGINT *(Activity Book page 128)*

Unscramble the words from the section "The Story of the Septuagint." Copy the letters in the numbered blocks to the blocks with the corresponding numbers at the bottom.

MOLTYPE	P T O L E M Y
DOL TSTENTEMA	O L D T E S T A M E N T
WEERBH	H E B R E W
NIOTARALSTN	T R A N S L A T I O N
REGKE	G R E E K
NETVEYS SISBERC	S E V E N T Y S C R I B E S
DOEGUNN	D U N G E O N
WIINTRG SDKE	W R I T I N G D E S K
RPPUSAY LRSCLO	P A P Y R U S S C R O L L
LILQU	Q U I L L
EDTIICANL	I D E N T I C A L

S E P T U A G I N T

CRAFT PROJECT: PHAROS LIGHTHOUSE

Materials:
- ☐ Colored sharpies
- ☐ 12 oz. solid white Styrofoam cup
- ☐ Small empty glass baby food jar
- ☐ Flameless (battery operated) tea light

Directions:

1. Using brown, black, and gray sharpies, create a brick pattern along the outside of the Styrofoam cup. Color the bricks using the different stone tones.
2. Turn the cup upside down and place it on a flat surface.
3. Turn the tea light on and place it in the baby food jar.
4. Put the lid on the jar and place the jar on top of the Styrofoam cup.
5. Enjoy!

CHAPTER 21
Greek Science

QUESTIONS FOR REVIEW:

1. **Who was the Greek scientist Euclid followed?**
Plato.

2. **What was Eratosthenes most known for?**
Figuring out the distance around the earth.

3. **What is geography?**
The study of the earth's surface and its features.

4. **What weapon did Archimedes invent to protect his homeland from attacking ships, and how did it work?**
He invented a giant heat ray which would use mirrors to reflect the sunlight at the ships, catching them on fire.

5. **What group of people eventually came in and conquered the Greeks?**
The Romans.

NARRATION EXERCISES:

Euclid

One of the most important Greek scientists and was a follower of the philosopher Plato. He came to Alexandria during the reign of Ptolemy to teach mathematics. While in Alexandria, Euclid wrote a textbook called *Elements*, a book that teaches geometry, which is the branch of math that deals with the shape, size, and position of objects. Euclid's book was very popular. It made things much easier for students to learn geometry. It was also a great help to engineers who designed buildings and anybody who built things. Elements became so popular that it was used as a textbook to teach geometry for over 2,000 years!

Archimedes

The greatest of all Greek scientists of the Hellenistic age. He was born in the Greek colony of Syracuse on the island of Sicily. No Greek scientist invented more clever devices or made more scientific discoveries than Archimedes. He built a heat ray to defend his home city of Syracuse. The ray worked by reflecting sun beams off giant mirrors and shooting them at enemy ships, which would catch them on fire. Archimedes also designed a giant crane with a hook that was big enough to pick up a ship. This, too, was used as a weapon. He nicknamed it the "Snatcher" because it could snatch enemy ships out of the water. But not everything Archimedes built was a weapon. He created a device that showed the position of the sun, moon, and planets that could be used to predict eclipses. He also discovered that by putting a screw inside a water-filled pipe, water could be pushed by turning the screw. This device is called "Archimedes' Screw" and was used by the Greeks to move water uphill. It is still used for this purpose today.

Activity Projects

MAP ACTIVITY: ALEXANDRIA, A CITY OF LEARNING
(Activity Book page 129)

1. Locate Greece and write "Euclid." With orange draw a line from Greece to Alexandria showing that Euclid came to Alexandria to teach mathematics. Draw math symbols in orange to represent Euclid's role in developing geometry.

2. Locate Athens and write "Eratosthenes" with green. Then draw a line down to Alexandria showing that he too came from Greece to Alexandria and became the chief librarian. Draw a book to indicate Eratosthenes' contribution.

3. Write "Archimedes" in red beside Syracuse and draw a line from Syracuse to Alexandria showing that Archimedes came to Alexandria to study. Draw a line in red back to Syracuse and draw a small screw to demonstrate one of Archimedes' many inventions.

COLORING PAGE

Archimedes *(Activity Book page 131)*

Color the picture of the Greek inventor Archimedes as he designs the "Archimedes Screw" which was used to move water.

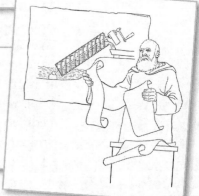

CRAFT PROJECT 1: PAPER MACHE GLOBE

- ☐ Flour and water (for paper mache glue)
- ☐ Round balloon
- ☐ Newspaper strips
- ☐ Paint (green, brown, blue, white, yellow)
- ☐ Paintbrushes
- ☐ Globe or atlas

Directions:

1. Using a spoon, mix your paper mache Glue using 1 part flour to 1 part water until you get a lump-free glue-like consistency. Add a little more water if it's too thick.

2. Blow up the balloon.

3. Place newspaper strips in the glue mixture and apply at least 3 coats thick to the outside of the balloon, allowing each layer to completely dry before applying the next.

4. Once dry, refer to your globe or atlas and paint your globe to match.

5. Make sure to talk about what a remarkable feat it was that Eratosthenes was able to be able to so closely calculate the distance around the world and that he is remembered as the father of geography.

6. Enjoy!

CRAFT PROJECT 2: ARCHIMEDES SCREW

Materials:

- ☐ Empty plastic water bottle
- ☐ Sharp knife (for adult use ONLY)
- ☐ Tack
- ☐ Hole punch
- ☐ Unsharpened pencil
- ☐ Clear packing tape
- ☐ 12 oz. glass
- ☐ Card stock paper
- ☐ Crispy rice cereal

Directions:

1. Cut the bottom off the water bottle.

2. Beginning just under the top of the water bottle (just below where the cap screws on) cut a triangle. The top point is below where the cap screws on and the bottom two points sit along the first ridge of the water bottle (1 1/2 inches total height).

3. Use the bottom of the glass and trace a circle on the card stock. You will make 7 circles all together.

4. Punch a hole through the middle of all the circles.

5. Cut a line from one side of each circle to the middle hole of the circle.

6. You will be pulling the cut ends in opposite directions and taping them to the next circle. See how the beginning of a screw is forming? Attach the other circles in the same fashion to form one continuous screw.

7. Place the pencil in the middle of the screw and secure each end with tape.

8. Place the screw in the plastic water bottle.

9. Place the tack through the cap of the water bottle and then into the eraser end of the pencil.

10. Place some crispy rice cereal in the open triangle at the bottle top.

11. Turn your screw to move the cereal from one end of the bottle to the other (you may want a bowl to catch the cereal as it exits).

12. Enjoy!

SCIENCE PROJECT: EUREKA! WATER DISPLACEMENT

Materials:
- ☐ Graduated cylinder or other means of measuring in milliliters (a newborn bottle will work)
- ☐ Food scale (something that weighs in grams)—in the absence of a scale, choose objects that you can look up the weight.
- ☐ Water
- ☐ 3-5 similar sized objects (maybe a penny, piece of aluminum foil wadded up, pebble, small piece of mulch … whatever you have handy).
- ☐ A calculator

Directions:
1. Pour some water into the cylinder and note the volume.
2. Immerse one object in the water (if it does not sink, it might need to be pushed under).
3. Measure the new volume and record the difference.
4. Repeat this process with all the objects.
5. Now calculate the density of each object. Density = Mass / Volume.
6. Enjoy!

CHAPTER 22
The Etruscans

QUESTIONS FOR REVIEW:

1. **What sort of shape does the country of Italy resemble?**
   A boot.

2. **What did the Etruscans leave behind in great amounts?**
   Jewelry.

3. **What form of architecture did the Etruscans make use of that allowed a building to hold more weight?**
   The arch.

4. **What were some of the things that might take place at an Etruscan funeral?**
   We know they featured boxing, chariot racing, and the killing of gladiators and slaves as sacrifices, among other strange traditions.

5. **What city does the chapter end with that would one day rule the world and change the destiny of all of Europe?**
   Rome.

NARRATION EXERCISES:

Etruscans

They lived in the Po Valley around 800 B.C. and ruled northern and central Italy, but left very little behind of their culture. One of the few things we learned about them was their love for jewelry. Archeologists found beautiful bracelets of hammered gold decorated with carvings of men and animals, jewel-studded necklaces, and lavishly decorated golden armbands. They also left behind wonderfully massive cities built out of enormous blocks of stone and surrounded by gigantic walls. The Etruscans were able to make such massive buildings by imploring the use of the arch, a rounded structure that spans a space—usually a door or gate. It is a wonderful invention that allows a building to hold much more weight. The arch was much sturdier than the Greek column. While almost all the Greek temples have long since tumbled to the ground, many Etruscan arches have survived to this day and are still in use. The Etruscans were also known for having wild and strange funerals that featured boxing matches, chariot racing, and the killing of gladiators and slaves as sacrifices, among other strange traditions.

Activity Projects

MAP ACTIVITY: ITALY *(Activity Book page 133)*

1. Locate Italy on your map and shade it green.
2. Write "Etruscans" along the northern end of Italy showing that they ruled this region.
3. Now locate the city of Rome in Italy and circle it in red. Write "Latins" above the city to show that it was governed by a wall tribe called the Latins.

COLORING PAGES

Gladiator *(Activity Book page 135)*

Color the picture of the Roman Gladiator who would've fought in the Colosseum.

MAZE: SEA VOYAGE TO ITALY

(Activity Book page 137) Travel through the maze. Imagine leaving the coast of Alexandria, passing the island of Crete, continuing along the coast of Africa, skirting around Sicily and finally reaching the land of Italy.

CRAFT PROJECT 1: ETRUSCAN GOLDEN BRACELET

Materials:
- ☐ Toilet paper tube
- ☐ Gold acrylic paint
- ☐ Paint brush
- ☐ Glue
- ☐ Aluminum foil
- ☐ Craft sand (if desired)

Directions:

1. Cut the toilet paper tube vertically so that it can be worn as a bracelet.
2. Trim the tube to desired width for your bracelet.
3. Glue a thinly rolled strip of aluminum foil to the top and bottom edges of the bracelet.
4. Use glue to create image on bracelet—could be person or animal or abstract image.
5. Sprinkle sand on glue and allow it to completely set OR use pieces of aluminum to decorate the bracelet.
6. Paint over the entire bracelet with the gold acrylic paint.
7. Enjoy!

CRAFT PROJECT 2: HOMEMADE BOXING GLOVES

Materials:
- ☐ Old pair of mittens or socks
- ☐ Thin foam
- ☐ Duct tape
- ☐ Scissors

Directions:

1. Cut foam to cover the back of your hand and wrap around your fingers.
2. Duct tape the foam to the mitten or sock.
3. Completely cover the sock or mitten with duct tape (loosely enough that your hand can go in and out).
4. Repeat steps to make second boxing glove.
5. Enjoy!

CHAPTER 23
The City of Seven Hills

QUESTIONS FOR REVIEW:

1. **What prince from the small tribe of Latins was Rome founded by?**
   Romulus.

2. **From whom did the Romans steal wives?**
   The Sabines.

3. **What Etruscan customs were brought to Rome when the Tarquins came to power?**
   Gladiator fights and the use of the arch in their architecture.

4. **What is a republic?**
   A form of government where officials elected by the people govern by the rule of laws, not the decrees of kings.

5. **Whose job was it to represent the plebeians in the republic?**
   The tribune.

NARRATION EXERCISES:

Patricians & Plebeians

Most of the land and wealth in the early republic of Rome was in the hands of the oldest and richest families, called the patricians. Those who were not from old families and did not have as much wealth were called plebeians. In the early republic, there were many laws that were not good for plebeians. For instance, many political offices were closed to plebeians. There were also laws that prohibited plebeians from marrying patricians. What made this worse was that only a tiny minority of Romans were patricians. Most Romans were plebeians, commoners who felt oppressed by a small minority. Eventually, the plebeians got so upset they walked out of Rome, resettling on a mountain outside Rome. The patricians didn't know what to do without the plebeians; Rome could not function without them. The patricians sent messengers to the plebeians, promising them more rights. They also created a new office called the tribune to represent the interests of the plebeians in the republic. The tribune had the power to stop any law from being passed if he thought it might hurt the plebeians. The plebeians were happy with this and returned to Rome. Though it took a long time for the plebeians to win their equality, all the old restrictions dropped away, and by 287 B.C. plebeians and patricians were mostly equal.

Activity Projects

MAP ACTIVITY: ROME *(Activity Book page 138)*

1. Locate Rome on the map. Draw a small hill and write "Romulus" above Rome showing that he was the first king of the small hilltop Rome. Circle Rome in orange then lightly shade the entire country indicating the spread of the Roman Empire to all of Italy by 264 B.C.

COLORING PAGES:

Romulus and Remus *(Activity Book page 139)*
Color the picture of brothers Romulus and Remus and the wolf who discovered and cared for them.

DRAMA PROJECT: ROLE PLAY

Choose to be either a patrician or plebeian and see if you can get someone else to play to other role. Think about life from your standpoint. Do you like the set-up of the republic? Why or why not? If you are the plebeian, would you have resettled in the mountains? If you are a patrician, would you have given them more representation? If you were a plebeian, would this representative, the tribune, have been enough for you to come back to Rome?

DOUBLE PUZZLE: A NEW WAY TO GOVERN *(Activity Book page 141)*

Unscramble the words from the section "A New Way to Govern." Copy the letters in the numbered blocks to the blocks with the corresponding numbers at the bottom.

TENNOMERGV	G O V E R N M E N T
TEEDELC	E L E C T E D
SIFLFIOCA	O F F I C I A L S
PEELOP VEORGN	P E O P L E G O V E R N
REUL FO WSAL	R U L E O F L A W S
TOW SOCSULN	T W O C O N S U L S
TESNEA	S E N A T E
LIBSAESEMS	A S S E M B L I E S
DESLIAE	A E D I L E S

R E P U B L I C
1 2 3 4 5 6 7 8

DRAWING PROJECT: ITALY

Materials:
- ☐ Drawing paper
- ☐ Pencil
- ☐ Eraser
- ☐ Colored pencils
- ☐ Template from Activity Book *(Activity Book page 142–144)*

Directions:
1. Use the template in the Activity book to instruct your child on how to draw Italy. Use whatever scale you want for your drawing.
2. Have your child locate and label Rome.
3. Color Italy.
4. Save this drawing for use in Chapter 24.
5. Enjoy!

CHAPTER 24
The Punic Wars

QUESTIONS FOR REVIEW:

1. **What island did Rome go to war with Carthage over?**
   Sicily.

2. **The Punic Wars got their name from the word "punici," which means what?**
   It was the Roman name for the Carthaginians.

3. **What did the Romans do well in the Punic wars that helped turn the momentum in their favor?**
   They learned from their enemy, studying the design of the Carthaginians ships and copying them, but improving them.

4. **What is a soldier who fights for whichever country pays him the most?**
   A mercenary.

5. **What animal did Hannibal make use of in his army to help them fight and cross over the Alps?**
   Elephants.

NARRATION EXERCISES:

Carthage

A city-state on the northern coast of Africa, directly across the sea from Italy, founded by the Phoenicians and the Canaanites of Tyre and Sidon. Because of its excellent location halfway across the Mediterranean, Carthage became wealthy and powerful, dominating shipping in the western Mediterranean and controlling territory from Africa to Spain. One place the Carthaginians tried to control was Sicily. They went to war with the Romans over this island just off the coast of Italy. These wars were called the Punic Wars, from the Latin word "punici," the Roman name for the Carthaginians.

Hannibal

The son of Hamilcar, the powerful general of the Carthaginian armies during the Punic Wars. After his defeat, Hamilcar taught Hannibal to hate the Romans. He would go on to become a powerful general like his father and ruled Spain for the Carthaginians. He finally launched his war on the Romans in 219 B.C. by attacking a Spanish city allied to Rome. He then made the bold decision to attack Rome, but to attack by climbing over the Alps instead of by sea. He used mercenaries to bulk up his army, and also implemented the use of battle elephants. The march over the treacherous mountains claimed the lives of many of his men, but eventually he reached the Po Valley and terrorized many Romans. Hannibal almost forced the Romans to surrender, but eventually a Roman general named Cornelius Scipio attacked Carthage. The forces of Scipio and Hannibal battled at a place called Zama, outside of Carthage, in the year 202 B.C. Scipio defeated Hannibal's army and the Carthaginians surrendered. Hannibal fled into exile, but the Romans pursued him. Hannibal eventually killed himself rather than be captured by the Romans.

Activity Projects

MAP ACTIVITY: PUNIC WARS - ROME'S VICTORY - 146 B.C.
(Activity Book page 145)

1. This map lays out the Empire of Rome at the end of the Punic Wars in the year 146 B.C.
2. Locate the following on the map and shade them red to show the Roman Empire in the year 146 B.C.: Italy, Sicily, Spain, Northern Africa, the southern coast of Gaul, Macedonia, and Greece.
3. Compare this map to the map from Chapter 23.
4. Look at how much the Roman Empire had expanded in just over a hundred years.

COLORING PAGE:

Hannibal *(Activity Book page 147)*

Color the picture of the Carthaginian general Hannibal and his battle elephants.

DRAWING PROJECT 1: ADD SICILY TO YOUR MAP FROM CHAPTER 23

Materials:
- ☐ Drawing paper
- ☐ Pencil
- ☐ Eraser
- ☐ Colored pencils
- ☐ Template from Activity Book *(Activity Book page 149)*

Directions:

1. Use the template in the Activity book to instruct your child on how to add Sicily to the Italy drawing. Use the same scale as you did for Italy.
2. Color Sicily.
3. Write "Punic Wars - Rome vs. Carthage" over Sicily.
4. Enjoy!

DRAWING PROJECT 2: WAR ELEPHANT

Materials:
- ☐ Drawing paper
- ☐ Pencil
- ☐ Eraser
- ☐ Colored pencils
- ☐ Template from Activity Book *(Activity Book page 150–152)*

Directions:

1. Use the template in the Activity book to instruct your child on how to draw an elephant. For more advanced artists, add in the war armor for the elephant.
2. Color your elephant.
3. Label your picture "Hannibal's battle-elephants."
4. Remind the child that many of Hannibal's men and elephants died on the long journey across the Alps.
5. Enjoy!

SNACK PROJECT: CHOCOLATE PEANUT ELEPHANT EARS

Ingredients:

- ☐ 1 pkg. frozen puff pastry
- ☐ Flour (to coat work surface)
- ☐ 1 egg
- ☐ 1 Tbsp. water
- ☐ 1/2 cup mini chocolate chips
- ☐ 1/4 cup crushed peanuts (more if desired)
- ☐ Parchment paper

Directions:

1. Thaw puff pastry dough.
2. Preheat oven to 400 degrees.
3. Beat egg and water.
4. Sprinkle work surface with flour.
5. Unfold pastry puff and brush it with the egg mixture.
6. Sprinkle 1/2 the chocolate chips and 1/2 the peanuts onto the pastry.
7. Lightly roll with a rolling pin so that the chocolate and peanuts are lightly embedded in the dough.
8. Fold the sides of the dough towards the center so that they go 1/2 way to the middle.
9. Fold again so that the 2 fold meet in the middle.
10. Then fold one last time 1/2 over 1/2 like closing a book.
11. Slice the dough into 1/2" slices and place the slices on a baking sheet.
12. Brush with egg mixture.
13. Bake approximately 8 minutes or until dough is light brown.
14. Enjoy!

CHAPTER 25
Greece and Rome Collide

QUESTIONS FOR REVIEW:

1. **What was a maniple? What was a legion?**

   A battle formation the Roman army used which consisted of 120 marching soldiers. Thirty maniples made up a legion.

2. **What did the Roman poet Horace mean when he said, "Captive Greece took Rome captive"?**

   That even though Rome conquered Greece, the Romans were so captivated by Greek culture and incorporated it into their lives so much, one might assume Greece had been the one to conquer Rome.

3. **Who was the leader of the Seleucid Empire at this time?**

   Antiochus III.

4. **Who did King Antiochus IV persecute after returning home and being embarrassed by Rome?**

   The Jewish people.

5. **What does "Maccabeus" mean?**

   The hammer.

NARRATION EXERCISES:

Legion

This was the backbone of the Roman army. It was a battle formation that consisted of thirty "maniples," which was a square of 120 soldiers marching into battle. The maniples could be moved forward or backward depending on how the battle was going. This made it very easy for the legions to move and respond to changes in battle—it made them more mobile. The phalanx, on the other hand, was very slow and difficult to move. The Roman legions with their maniples easily outmaneuvered and destroyed the Macedonian phalanx.

The Maccabees

This Jewish family stood up to King Antiochus IV of the Seleucid Empire when he began to persecute them. Antiochus forbid them to worship the God of their fathers, ordered their Scriptures burned, and forced them to sacrifice to the Greek gods and eat Greek foods—foods prohibited by the Law of Moses. Jews who refused to submit to Antiochus' laws were killed. But a man named Mattathias and his sons refused to obey Antiochus or worship the Greek gods. They fled to the hills of Judea, taking many other Jewish men with them. These Jews started attacking the troops of Antiochus. They were led by Mattathias' son, Judas. Judas won so many victories against Antiochus that he was nicknamed "Maccabeus," which means "the hammer." His family was called the Maccabees. The Maccabees would go on to do great things for the Jewish people, including capturing Jerusalem. Eventually, they made an alliance with Rome to help protect the Jewish people in exchange for allegiance to the Romans.

Activity Projects

MAP ACTIVITY: THE MACCABEES *(Activity Book page 153)*

1. Locate Judea and draw a few hill tops using a brown colored pencil. This is the land to which the Maccabees fled.
2. Locate Jerusalem and circle it with yellow, indicating the Maccabees were victorious at taking the city.
3. Beside Jerusalem draw a statue and mark through it with a red "x" showing that the Maccabees threw out the statues of the Greek gods.
4. Draw a temple and circle it with yellow showing that the Maccabees rededicated the temple to the worship of the one, true God.

COLORING PAGE:

Judas Maccabeus *(Activity Book page 155)*

Color the picture of the Jewish rebel named Judas who stood up to King Antiochus IV and was nicknamed "the hammer."

ACTIVITY PROJECT: MANIPLE VS. PHALANX CHECKERS

Materials:
- ☐ Activity Book pages for game board and pieces *(Activity Book page 157–159)*
- ☐ Coloring pencils
- ☐ Scissors
- ☐ Tape

Directions:

1. Tear out the two pages for your game board and cut them along the border. Tape them together along the underside to create the game board.
2. Color your pieces. Spears represent the phalanx team and shields represent the maniple team.
3. The player with the maniple pieces gets the first move since we know the maniples moved more easily.
4. Play the game according to standard checker play.
5. Enjoy!

CRAFT PROJECT 1: WALKING STICK FOR THE OLD MAN WHO FACED THE ARMY

Materials:
- ☐ Solid wood stick appropriate for the height of the student.
- ☐ Sanding paper
- ☐ Drill
- ☐ Leather cord
- ☐ Craft beads for decoration

Directions:

1. Find a stick appropriate for the height of the student.
2. Begin by knocking off any larger pieces of bark.
3. Using hand sanding paper, sand the entire stick until completely smooth.
4. An adult should drill a hole 3 inches from the top of the stick. The hole should be just thick enough for your cord to fit through.
5. Run the leather cord through the hole and knot on one end so that it cannot slip out of the hole.
6. Place beads on the cord and knot at the end to keep the beads in place.
7. Enjoy!

CRAFT PROJECT 2: MAKE A HAMMER TO REPRESENT MACCABEUS

Materials:
- ☐ Empty small oatmeal container (either cylinder or box will work here)
- ☐ Paper towel tube
- ☐ Duct tape
- ☐ Primer paint / white paint
- ☐ Silver or grey paint
- ☐ Brown paint
- ☐ Leather cord
- ☐ Hot glue gun
- ☐ Pencil
- ☐ X-acto knife

Directions:

1. Place the end of the paper towel tube on the side of the oatmeal container and trace the circle.

2. An adult should use an X-acto knife to cut out the circle.

3. Slide the paper towel tube into the oatmeal container and secure it with duct tape.

4. Paint the outside of the oatmeal container with primer and then with the silver or grey paint.

5. Paint the toilet paper tube brown if desired.

6. Wrap the leather cord around the hammer. Do your best to hide your duct tape.

7. Hot glue to top and bottom of the cord to secure it in place.

8. Enjoy!

CHAPTER 26
Marius and Sulla

QUESTIONS FOR REVIEW:

1. **Who took over the farms of the Roman soldiers while they were gone fighting wars?**

   Senators and wealthy Romans bought up all the land of the farmers/soldiers who were away at battle.

2. **What was a latifundia?**

   A large farm owned by Roman Senators and run by slaves.

3. **What was the name of the bill that Tiberius Gracchus proposed that would break up the latifundias and give the farms back to the poor Romans?**

   The Land Bill.

4. **What did the young Gaius Marius find on the cliff side that he saw as a miraculous sign?**

   Seven eagle eggs in a nest.

5. **What is a civil war?**

   When a country fights amongst itself rather than against a foreign land.

NARRATION EXERCISES:

The Land Bill

During the long stretch of wars the Romans fought, many of the farmers who were also soldiers were off at battle. While they were gone, Roman Senators and other wealthy Romans bought up their farms, creating latifundias, which were large farms run by slaves. When the soldiers returned home, they found much of their land gone. In 133 B.C., a man named Tiberius Gracchus was elected tribune. Tiberius said the republic should pass a law breaking up the large latifundia and give the land back to the poor Romans. This was called the Land Bill. Many people liked Gracchus' Land Bill; it would restore property to those who had fought for Rome. But the wealthy and many of the Senators were very much opposed to it. The Land Bill would take away a lot of their wealth. Those who supported the Land Bill were known as the Populares; those who were against the Land Bill were known as the Optimates. There was much conflict and strife in the years following the proposal of the Land Bill, so much that eventually Rome would become engaged in a civil war.

Cornelius Sulla

He was a general in the Roman army that the Senate gave command to when they were upset at the power Gaius Marius had seized. Marius was allowed to be consul many times in a row because of his popularity, but this was illegal under the Roman constitution. Eventually, people started to resent him, especially wealthy Romans. Sulla was an Optimate and friend of the Senate and so they elected him to take down Marius. Sulla gathered six Roman legions and marched on Rome. A bitter struggled ensued between the two men and their followers, but eventually Sulla was victorious and was made dictator of Rome. Sulla executed everybody that had anything to do with Marius and the populares. He may have killed as many as 9,000 people. After Sulla had killed enough populares, he resigned from the office of dictator in the year 81 B.C. Then he retired to his mansion to write a story about his life. He died peacefully a few years later. The Romans nicknamed Sulla "Felix," which means "the happy one," because they believe he had lived a very happy and successful life.

Activity Projects

MAP ACTIVITY: ROME DIVIDED *(Activity Book page 161)*

1. Circle Rome with yellow and draw a line down the middle.
2. Color one half red and draw arrows from the outside of the circle headed into the city. Label this "Sulla."
3. Color the other half blue and draw arrows from the outside of the circle heading into the city. Label this "Marius."
4. Above the city write "civil war."

DRAMA PROJECT: FARMER VS. SENATOR DEBATE

Directions:

Have a debate between a Roman farmer who has been at war and a Roman Senator who bought up his land while he was away. Discuss the Land Bill and why you are for or against it. Were you among the Populares or Optimates?

DRAWING PROJECT: EAGLE'S HEAD

Materials:
- ☐ Drawing paper
- ☐ Pencil
- ☐ Eraser
- ☐ Colored pencils
- ☐ Template from Activity Book
  (Activity Book page 162–163)

Directions:

1. Use the template in the Activity Book to instruct your child on how to draw an eagle's head.
2. Color as desired.
3. Remind the student of the nest that Marius saw and how he made the eagle the official symbol of the Roman republic and the Roman army.
4. Enjoy!

SNACK PROJECT: GAIUS MARIUS EAGLE'S EGGS IN A NEST

Ingredients:
- ☐ 1 pkg. semi-sweet/milk chocolate chips
- ☐ 1/2 cup peanut butter
- ☐ 4 cups chow mein noodles
- ☐ 1 package jelly beans

Directions:

1. Microwave chocolate chips on medium-high for 1 minute or until slightly melted.
2. Stir in peanut butter.
3. Stir in chow mein noodles.
4. Using a serving size spoon, dish out heaping spoonfuls onto wax paper and form into nest shape.
5. Refrigerate until ready to serve.
6. Place 7 jelly beans in each nest—the 7 eggs Gaius Marius saw and took as a miraculous sign.
7. Enjoy!

CHAPTER 27
The Rise and Fall of Julius Caesar

QUESTIONS FOR REVIEW:

1. **What is a triumph?**

   Huge parades given to conquering generals.

2. **Who was Julius Caesar's uncle?**

   Gaius Marius.

3. **What did Caesar do when he learned of Pompey's death, who was his enemy?**

   He had him buried with respect and allowed a statue to be built in his honor.

4. **Who did Caesar fall in love with while in Alexandria?**

   Cleopatra, the sister of the Egyptian King Ptolemy XIII.

5. **How did Julius Caesar die?**

   Roman Senators, including some of his friends, murdered him by stabbing him many times.

NARRATION EXERCISES:

Julius Caesar

The nephew of Gaius Marius, Julius Caesar became an important general in the Roman army. He led his troops to many victories in Gaul and Britain and returned home a hero. He then built Rome a new harbor, improved public buildings, and even gave money to the people. Caesar also offered the poorer class free land in Rome's newly conquered territories overseas. All this made Caesar extremely well-liked; with popularity he came to power. Soon, he would clash with Pompey, a fellow Roman general, in a fight over power. Caesar would eventually win. His conquest took him to Egypt where he fell in love with the King's sister, Cleopatra. He helped her overthrow her brother so that she could rule Egypt while Caesar ruled Rome. Caesar went on to defeat Pompey's supporters all over the world, including in Spain and Africa. But he eventually pardoned most of Pompey's supporters back in Rome, and tried to rule peacefully after appointing himself dictator for life. Though Caesar was popular, not everyone liked him. He was eventually killed by several Roman senators, including some of his friends, when they stabbed him to death.

Cleopatra

The sister of the King of Egypt, Ptolemy XIII. She fell in love with Julius Caesar and with his help overthrew her brother to become the sole ruler of Egypt. After Caesar's death, his best friend, Marc Antony, fell in love with her and lived with her in Alexandria. Marc Antony was at that time locked in a struggle to rule Rome with Gaius Octavian, Caesar's nephew. Marc Antony and Cleopatra made plans to rule Egypt and unite it with Rome. But Octavian raised a navy and sailed to Egypt and destroyed the forces of Marc Antony and Cleopatra. Marc Antony killed himself, while Cleopatra tried to make Octavian fall in love with her. But he wanted no part of her and said that he would take her prisoner back to Rome. Before this could happen, according to legend, she had one of her maids bring her a cobra hidden in a basket. Cleopatra let the cobra bite her and died from the poison.

Activity Projects

MAP ACTIVITY: JULIUS CAESAR VS. POMPEY THE GREAT
(Activity Book page 164)

1. Locate the Rubicon River and trace it with blue.
2. Use a yellow colored pencil and draw arrows from the Rubicon River south to Rome and label this "Caesar."
3. Circle Rome in red and write "4 years" beside it indicating the battle lasted for 4 years.
4. With green, draw arrows south to Egypt indicating Pompey's retreat to Egypt and label this "Pompey."

COLORING PAGE:

Cleopatra *(Activity Book page 165)*

Color the picture of the Egyptian ruler, Cleopatra, as she sits on her throne.

CROSSWORD PUZZLE: JULIUS CAESAR *(Activity Book page 167)*

Across:
4. pardon
5. Ptolemy
6. Marc Antony
7. dictator

Down:
1. plebeians
2. Cleopatra
3. Gaul
4. Pompey

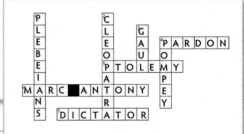

CRAFT PROJECT: MAKE A COBRA

Materials:
- ☐ Construction paper in the colors you want for your snake
- ☐ Stapler or clear tape
- ☐ Googly eyes
- ☐ Craft glue
- ☐ Small piece of red construction paper (for tongue)
- ☐ Plastic straw

Directions:
1. Cut 8" x 2" strips from the construction paper.
2. Staple or tape the first strip into a loop.
3. Connect the second loop to the first and continue on until snake is of desired length (this will form a paper chain).
4. Cut 2, 2 inch x 4 inch strips of construction paper.
5. Cut a 4 inch segment from the plastic straw.
6. Tape the straw to the back of the first strip of paper and then tape the other strip on the backside to completely cover the straw.
7. Attach this strip enforced by the straw to the first loop in the chain (this will be the cobra standing up).
8. Add one more loop to the top of the straw (the cobra's head).
9. Cut a small rectangle from red construction paper and cut a slit at one end. Attach to the head of your snake (this will be the snake's tongue).

10. Glue googly eyes above the tongue.

11. Cut a heart shape and tape it to the back of the head. This will distinguish it as a cobra.

12. Enjoy!

CHAPTER 28
The Coming of Christ

QUESTIONS FOR REVIEW:

1. **What was the Incarnation and what does that word mean?**

   This was when God became man. Incarnation comes from two Latin words that mean "to become flesh."

2. **What does "Christ" mean in Greek?**

   Messiah.

3. **What does "apostle" mean in Greek?**

   Messenger.

4. **Why did Jesus compare Himself to a shepherd?**

   He compared mankind to His flock who had strayed from Him, and He came to earth to lead them back to God the way a shepherd watches over his flock.

5. **What group of people hated Jesus and wanted Him killed?**

   The Pharisees.

NARRATION EXERCISES:

The Incarnation

This was the act of God becoming man. In Jesus, God became flesh when the Holy Spirit descended upon Mary. Jesus came down from heaven and became a person without ceasing to be God. The word "Incarnation" in Greek comes from two Latin words that mean "to become flesh." The Incarnation was the most important event that ever occurred in the history of the world. It is the only time God has ever visited earth in the flesh to speak to man. People today all over the world measure their time from the Incarnation. The years before the Incarnation are B.C. ("Before Christ") and those years after Jesus' birth are called A.D. ("Anno Domini," Latin for "year of our Lord"). Therefore, we measure all things that happened on this event.

The Crucifixion

Although Jesus had gained many followers throughout His ministry, the Pharisees wanted Him dead. When Jesus was in Jerusalem with His followers celebrating the Jewish feast of Passover, the Pharisees paid one of Jesus' followers, Judas, to betray Him. After being handed over, Jesus was condemned to death because they believed He was teaching people to disobey the Law of Moses. But the Jews could not execute anybody; that was reserved for the Romans who governed Judea. The Pharisees handed Jesus over to the Roman governor, Pontius Pilate. They told Pilate that Jesus was a traitor and a danger to the Roman state. Pilate did not understand and would have let Jesus go, but the Pharisees demanded His death, and Pilate feared an uprising from the angry mob who was shouting, "Crucify Him! Crucify Him!" Finally, Pilate relented and ordered Jesus crucified. Jesus was whipped and then made to carry His cross to a place outside Jerusalem called Golgotha, which means, "place of the skull." It was a hill more commonly known today as Calvary. On this hill Jesus was crucified between two thieves as his weeping mother stood watching. The traditional date of Jesus' death is 33 A.D.

Activity Projects

MAP ACTIVITY: JESUS *(Activity Book page 169)*

1. Locate Bethlehem on the map and with yellow draw a star above it indicating this is where Jesus was born.
2. Locate the province of Galilee and shade it with blue. This is where Jesus began preaching.
3. Circle Jerusalem in red. This is where Jesus preached in the temple, a message that the Pharisees were not fond of. It is also where Judas betrayed Jesus.
4. Color the inside of the circle yellow. Although this city was the place that Jesus was condemned, it is also the place that He instituted the Eucharist and the place that he offered himself as a sacrifice.
5. To the side of Jerusalem draw a hill with a cross atop it to represent Golgotha, commonly known today at Calvary.

CROSSWORD PUZZLE: THE MESSIAH *(Activity Book page 170)*

Across:
- 3. God
- 7. Eucharist
- 12. Galilee
- 13. Shepherd
- 14. Pharisees

Down:
- 1. Apostle
- 2. twelve
- 4. Crucify Him
- 5. Mary
- 6. sinless
- 8. Christ
- 9. Joseph
- 10. David
- 11. Caesar
- 15. Augustus

CRAFT PROJECT 1: NATIVITY STAINED GLASS

Materials:
- ☐ Template from Activity Book *(Activity Book page 171)*
- ☐ Black construction paper
- ☐ Tape
- ☐ Scissors
- ☐ Tissue paper in various colors
- ☐ Contact paper

Directions:

1. Cut various colors of tissue paper into 1 inch squares.

2. Using your template from the Activity Book, cut out the nativity scene using the black construction paper.

3. Cut a piece of contact paper large enough to cover the nativity scene and lay in sticky side up on a flat surface.

4. Place the black nativity scene on the contact paper.

5. Place the squares on the contact paper, completely covering it.

6. Place a second piece of contact paper on the tissue / nativity scene beginning at one corner and carefully working your way to the opposite corner. Take care to press out all air along the way.

7. Trim off all the excess contact paper.

8. Enjoy!

CHAPTER 29
Fishers of Men

QUESTIONS FOR REVIEW:

1. **Who was first to encounter the risen Christ?**
   Mary Magdalen and several other women.

2. **What is the day called when the Holy Spirit descended upon the apostles?**
   Pentecost.

3. **Who was the head of the apostles?**
   Peter.

4. **What does the word "Christian" mean?**
   Christ-like.

5. **What does Catholic mean?**
   Universal.

NARRATION EXERCISES:

St. Paul

He was one of the most important of the apostles, but was not one of the first twelve. For a time, he hated Christians and tried to kill them. But one day the Lord Jesus appeared to him on the road to Damascus. Shining amidst a blaze of light, Jesus told Paul that he was to take the Gospel to the nations and their kings. At first, the apostles did not trust Paul; they knew him only as a persecutor of Christians. But when he told them how the Lord appeared to him and how he had even been beaten for his belief in Jesus, they accepted him. While the other apostles preached mainly among Jews, Paul preached to the non-Jews. He traveled all over the Roman Empire, from Jerusalem to Asia Minor and Greece, to Macedonia, Italy, Malta, and even as far away as Spain. Everywhere he went, men and women listened to the Gospel eagerly and became Christians.

The Early Church

After several decades, the apostles and the whole first generation of Christians died. Sometimes they died violently. Most of the apostles were martyrs, people who died at the hands of the Romans for the sake of a belief. The Christians always remembered the martyrs and honored their memory by celebrating Mass at their tombs every year on the anniversary of their death. The early Church had no buildings. Wealthy Christians often converted their houses into places of worship; Mass was said in these house-churches. The Church in each city was governed by a bishop, who would sometimes ordain other men to help him in his ministry. These men were called presbyters, or priests. Deacons were also ordained for the purpose of distributing money to the poor and helping sick members of the church. The Christian faith was a faith that spread in secret, for fear of what the Romans would do to them, but by 100 A.D., around the time the last apostle died, most cities throughout the Roman Empire had Christian churches in them. The Catholic Church was governed by bishops in each city, all in union with the successor of Peter in Rome. The churches were small, and most kept to themselves, but they were slowly growing. Even occasional persecutions did not halt their growth; in fact, persecution often led to more people converting.

Activity Projects

MAP ACTIVITY: THE ASCENSION *(Activity Book page 173)*

1. Locate the city of Jerusalem.
2. To the right of the city, where the Mount of Olives is located, draw Jesus with arrows pointed up. This shows the ascension of Jesus.
3. Talk about Jesus' ascension occurring at a very specific place and time. It is a historical fact and was witnessed by many people.

COLORING PAGE:

Pentecost *(Activity Book page 175)*

Color the picture of the Holy Spirit descending upon the apostle Peter.

WORD SEARCH: FISHERS OF MEN

(Activity Book page 177) Locate and circle all of the words from the word bank. Encourage your student to recount Jesus' life, death, and resurrection as these key words are found.

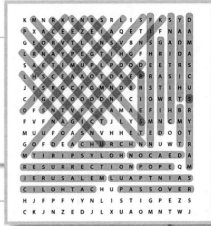

DOUBLE PUZZLE: PENTECOST

(Activity Book page 178) Unscramble the words from the section "Pentecost." Copy the letters in the numbered blocks to the blocks with the corresponding numbers at the bottom.

CRAFT PROJECT: FISHING POLE— FISHERS OF MEN

Materials:
- ☐ Template in Activity Book *(Activity Book page 179)*
- ☐ 18 inch stick
- ☐ Scissors
- ☐ Colored pencils
- ☐ Tape
- ☐ Hole punch
- ☐ 18 inch piece of string

Directions:

1. Color the man and woman in the template and cut them out.

2. Hole punch the shoulder or head of each figure.

3. Wrap the 18 inch piece of string around one end of the stick several times and tie off (leaving the majority of the string hanging off the end). Tape around the string to secure it.

4. Tie the other end of the sting through the hole punch.

5. Discuss that the apostles, many of whom began as fishermen, are now fishers of men. They are to "Go and make disciples of all nations." Just so, we too are to be fishers of men for Christ, catching souls for the kingdom of heaven!

SCIENCE PROJECT: COLORING THE WORLD—THE SPREAD OF CHRISTIANITY

Materials:
- ☐ Milk
- ☐ Pie plate
- ☐ Food coloring
- ☐ Dish soap
- ☐ Cotton swab

Directions:

1. Pour the milk onto the dinner plate so that it is at least ? inch deep.
2. Put a single drop of each color of food coloring in the center of the plate of milk.
3. Dip one end of the cotton swab in dish soap so that it is completely covered.
4. Touch the center of the plate of milk with the dish soap end of the cotton swab.
5. See how the colors spread and discuss how Christianity spread throughout the world.

CHAPTER 30
Life Under the Julio-Claudians

QUESTIONS FOR REVIEW:

1. The word Imperator means "he who holds power." What word do we derive from it?

   Emperor.

2. Who was emperor when Jesus was crucified?

   Tiberius Caesar.

3. Who was the cruel and insane Roman emperor who persecuted the Christians and had Sts. Peter and Paul killed?

   Nero.

4. What did the Romans call a country farm home?

   A villa.

5. Why did wealthy Romans leave Rome for the summer?

   The heat was unbearable and caused a stench in the streets from the sweaty people and rotting garbage.

NARRATION EXERCISES:

Nero

He became the emperor of Rome when he was only 17. His mother married the emperor, poisoned him, and killed his son so that Nero could become the ruler of Rome. He was partially mad and very cruel. He killed many members of his family, including his mother and wife. Nero also persecuted Christians. In 64 A.D., a great fire broke out in Rome. Nero blamed the Christians for the fire. He had many arrested and crucified or thrown to wild beasts. According to tradition, both St. Peter and St. Paul were killed in this persecution. Peter was crucified upside down and Paul was beheaded. Under Nero, Rome lost several battles on its frontiers. The Roman legions grew restless and the Roman people groaned under his oppression. In the year 68 A.D., a Roman general from Spain named Galba revolted and marched on Rome. Nero's guards and supporters deserted him. Nero fled to a stable outside Rome where he killed himself. The Julio-Claudian line ended with the death of Nero.

Clients and Patrons

Most people in Roman society were either clients or patrons. Patrons were important men who had money, power, and influence in society. Clients were less well-off people who needed the help of their patrons. Patrons and clients assisted one another; patrons helped their clients with their difficulties, and clients often ran errands for their patrons.

Activity Projects

CRYPTOGRAM: TITLES FOR OCTAVIAN

Code chosen at random

(Activity Book page 181) **Use the section "The First Roman Emperor" to decode the titles given to Octavian.**

   Answer: Princeps, Augustus, Pater Patriae, Divi Filius, Imperator

CROSSWORD PUZZLE: THE JULIO-CLAUDIANS *(Activity Book page 182)*

Across:
1. Caligula
4. Claudius
6. Tiberius
7. Agrippina
8. Livia

Down:
2. Augustus Caesar
3. Julio-Claudians
5. Nero

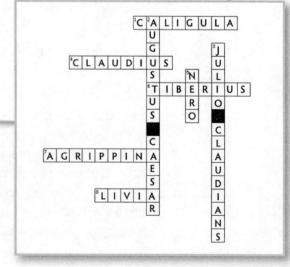

CRAFT PROJECT: LAUREL WREATH FOR AUGUSTUS CAESAR

Materials:
- ☐ Plastic headband
- ☐ Green construction paper
- ☐ Hot glue
- ☐ Scissors

Directions:

1. Cut out 30–40 2 inch long leaves from the green construction paper.
2. Hot glue them to the headband so that leaves go on both sides of the headband.
3. Wear the headband over the back of the head. (Think of wearing sunglasses only on the backside of your head.)
4. Enjoy!

CHAPTER 31
Five "Good" Emperors

QUESTIONS FOR REVIEW:

1. **Who oversaw the construction of the famous Colosseum in Rome?**
   Vespasian.

2. **What were some of the events held in the Colosseum?**
   Gladiator fights and races, as well as pretend ship battles when they flooded the arena with water.

3. **What was unusual about the way the five "good" emperors were selected?**
   They were not family, fathers and sons passing down power, but rather a group of different men adopting their successor.

4. **What did the Romans call someone from outside the Roman Empire who did not have Roman culture and were constantly trying to invade Rome?**
   A barbarian.

5. **Though these emperors were considered good by the Romans, who did not find their rule just and peaceful?**
   The Christians, who were persecuted and killed by all five of the "good" emperors.

NARRATION EXERCISES:

Five "Good" Emperors

After the death of Domitian, Vespasian's son, the Senate came together and did something that had never been done before—selected one of their own to be the emperor, a senator named Nerva. But Nerva was old, childless, and soon grew sick. If he died without an heir, the empire might again fall into chaos. Nerva chose a Spanish general named Trajan to be his successor and left him the throne. With Nerva began the reigns of what are called the "Five Good Emperors." The Five Good Emperors were Nerva, Trajan, Hadrian, Antoninus Pius, and Marcus Aurelius. None of them were related to each other. As Nerva had adopted Trajan, each one adopted their successor. They reigned from 98 A.D. to 180 A.D. They were called "good" because under their rule, Rome conquered even more territory and expanded its power further, and they were good at governing. Rather than satisfy their own pleasures or rob the people, they worked tirelessly to make the Roman Empire a better place to live. But not everyone thought they were "good." The Christians were persecuted and killed during this period of the five "good" emperors.

St. Ignatius of Antioch

He was a bishop of the early Church and was a man who once knew St. Peter. Ignatius was a martyr for the faith, having been fed to wild beasts in the Colosseum for refusing to worship the Roman gods. But Ignatius met his death with faith and courage. He wrote while awaiting his execution, "I am the wheat of God. I am ground by the teeth of the wild beasts, that I may be found to be the pure bread of Christ."

Activity Projects

MAP ACTIVITY: SAINT IGNATIUS *(Activity Book page 183)*

1. Locate Syria on the map and circle it in red. This is where Trajan questioned Saint Ignatius and had him arrested.
2. Shade the Mediterranean Sea blue.
3. Using red, draw a line from Syria through the Mediterranean Sea and up to Rome showing that Trajan had Saint Ignatius sent to Rome.
4. Circle Rome with red.
5. Draw a stalk of wheat beside Rome showing that Saint Ignatius said "I am the wheat of God … I am ground by the teeth of the wild beasts, that I may be found to be the pure great of Christ."

COLORING PAGE:

Barbarian *(Activity Book page 185)*

Color the picture of the barbarian as he moves to invade Rome.

WORD SEARCH: THE FIVE "GOOD" EMPERORS

(Activity Book page 187–188)

1. Vespasian
2. Colosseum
3. Gladiator
4. Nerva
5. Trajan
6. Hadrian
7. Antoninus Pius
8. Marcus Aurelius
9. Rome
10. Germany
11. adopted
12. good emperors
13. law
14. justice
15. peace
16. barbarian
17. Christian
18. death
19. Saint Ignatius
20. Commodus

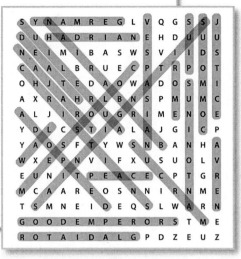

MAZE: HELP THE GLADIATOR KILL THE WILD BEASTS AND ESCAPE THE COLOSSEUM

(Activity Book page 189) Can you help the gladiator escape the Colosseum?

CRAFT PROJECT: WILD BEASTS AT THE COLOSSEUM—LION

Materials:

☐ Paper plate
☐ Orange paint
☐ Yellow paint
☐ Googly eyes
☐ Black marker
☐ Scissors

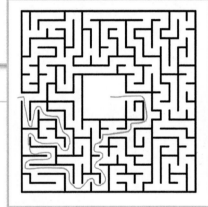

Directions:

1. Paint the outer rim of the paper plate orange.
2. Paint the inner circle of the paper plate yellow. The orange and yellow should meet at the edge of the inner circle.
3. Allow paint to fully dry.
4. Cut 1/4" slits all along the orange outer rim to create the mane for the lion.
5. Add googly eyes.
6. Make a triangle nose for the lion and add 3 whiskers per side.
7. Add a mouth.
8. Enjoy!

CHAPTER 32
Collapse

QUESTIONS FOR REVIEW:

1. From what did a Roman emperor need support in order to rule and have complete control?

   The army.

2. Who often invaded Roman lands from Germany to the north?

   Barbarians.

3. Why did the persecution of Christians weaken Rome?

   Because the Christians were often the hardest working people in society.

4. The emperor Aurelian tried to make all Romans, including Christians, worship the sun. What was the name of this sun god?

   Sol Invictus.

5. How was Aurelian killed?

   He was murdered by his own troops on his way to conquer Persia.

NARRATION EXERCISES:

Barbarians

This was the term Romans gave to outside invaders who did not have Roman culture. They most often came from Germany, but also Asia. They spent years attempting to attack Rome, wanting good lands to live on. Whenever barbarians passed through the land, everything was thrown into disorder. They sacked farms and overtook towns. Of the most well known German barbarian tribes were the Visigoths, Ostrogoths, Vandals, Franks, Alemanni, Saxons, and the Lombards. These tribes poured into Roman lands from the north and east. The barbarian invasions made life difficult for the Romans. The war and conflict disrupted farming and trading. Money became scarce and the prices of food and cloth went up. It was hard for people to get by, and many throughout the Roman Empire became poor.

Aurelian

He became emperor in the year 270 A.D. after serving in the military under three prior emperors. Like most other emperors of the day, he took power by overthrowing the previous emperor. Aurelian was a strong man and a good leader. He knew the empire was in trouble and had a plan for restoring it. He won several important victories over the barbarians before recapturing Gaul. He also defeated the armies of Zenobia and took back all the lands under Palmyra. Aurelian built massive walls around the city of Rome to make sure the capital was defended. Aurelian believed the empire needed unity more than anything else, so he ordered all the people in the empire to worship the sun under the title Sol Invictus ("Unconquerable Sun"). Aurelian wanted only one faith for the empire and organized persecutions against Christians who would not worship the sun. After all his success in war, Aurelian decided the time was right to attack Persia. He began marching east in 275 A.D., but never arrived. His soldiers murdered him on the way and the empire was again plunged into chaos.

Activity Projects

MAP ACTIVITY: BARBARIAN INVASIONS *(Activity Book page 190)*

1. Locate the Germanic tribes and circle them in green. Draw an arrow from the Germanic tribes south to Rome showing their invasion from the north.

2. Locate Asia and circle it in purple. Draw an arrow from Asia west to Rome showing their invasion from the east.

3. Shade the land around Rome red to indicate that it was under attack from all over.

4. Locate Gaul and Britain and shade them yellow showing that when the Roman emperors could not defend this region from barbarian attacks, it broke from Rome and Postumus ruled it as its own little kingdom.

WORD SEARCH: BARBARIAN INVASIONS

(Activity Book page 191) Locate and circle all of the words from the word bank. This is primarily a list of the barbarian invaders, another opportunity to see the names of the barbarian tribes so as to help memorize them.

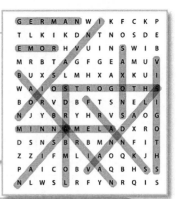

CRAFT PROJECT 1: ANIMAL SKIN VEST FOR A BARBARIAN

Materials:
- ☐ Paper grocery bag
- ☐ Scissors
- ☐ Oil pastel paints or markers
- ☐ Paint brush (if applicable)
- ☐ Craft faux fur (if desired)
- ☐ Hot glue gun (if applicable)

Directions:

1. With the bag folded flat, cut a straight line up the middle of one side (where the vest will open).
2. Cut a head hole in the bottom of the bag.
3. Cut an arm hole on either side of the bag.
4. Crumple the bag and flatten and repeat 4-5 times, smoothing in between each crumple so that new creases are formed each time. This will give the bag the animal hide look.
5. Now … you have some options: Easy level: Use markers to make spots or stripes for your animal skin. Medium level: Use oil pastels to create spots or stripes for your animal hide and allow to fully dry. More difficult: Use oil pastels to create spots or stripes for your animal hide and fully dry. Then, cut sections from the faux fur and hot glue them on as desired.
6. Enjoy!

CRAFT PROJECT 2: THE CROWN OF THE CHRISTIAN MARTYRS

Materials:
- ☐ Red or white 9 inch diameter paper plate
- ☐ Red crayon or marker if using paper plate
- ☐ Scissors

☐ Hot glue
☐ Craft gems

Directions:

1. If using a white plate, completely color your plate red.
2. Fold the plate in half.
3. Hold the plate as if it is a protractor.
4. Cut a slit directly up at 90 degrees stopping before the outer rim of the plate.
5. Cut 2 slits each at the 45 degree marks stopping at the outer rim of the plate.
6. Open the plate and cut a slit straight across at what would be the 180 degree mark.
7. Hot glue gems to each triangular tip.
8. The plate should fit over the head (you can increase the length of the slits if it's too tight).
9. Enjoy!

CHAPTER 33
The Growth of the Catholic Church

QUESTIONS FOR REVIEW:

1. **What did Jesus compare the Church to?**

   A tree that starts with a tiny seed and grows strong and healthy.

2. **What is an apologist?**

   A writer who tried to explain Christianity to the pagans.

3. **What is the study of God and His revelation called?**

   Theology

4. **What were some of the issues early Catholics disagreed over?**

   Whether or not Jesus was equal to God the Father; which sins could the Church could forgive and which they could not forgive; and was baptism valid if done by someone other than the Church's ordained ministers.

5. **What is a heresy?**

   Teachings other than those accepted by the Church. Heresy is a Greek word that means "wrong thinking."

NARRATION EXERCISES:

St. Justin Martyr

He was one of the first and greatest Christian apologists. He wrote during the time of Emperors Hadrian and Antoninus Pius. St. Justin explained that the Christians did not do any of the evil things the Roman leaders accused them of, and that they were among some of the most loyal subjects in the empire. He argued the emperors should change the laws against Christians. St. Justin also offered one of the earliest written records of what Christian worship was like in describing the Mass. But

St. Justin's apologies did not convince the emperors. He was handed over to the authorities and beheaded around the year 167 A.D.

Christian Theology

As Christians explained their faith to pagans and discussed it with each other, their ideas developed. This was the beginning of Christian theology. Theology is the science or study of God and His revelation. Those who studied and wrote about Christian theology were called theologians. Some theologians were also apologists, some were bishops, and others were just lay people with a passion for writing and speaking about God. They helped resolve conflicts that arose amongst the early Christians. Theologians would write letters making their arguments for their side. Some of the great theologians of the early Church were St. Justin Martyr, St. Cyprian of Carthage, and St. Irenaeus of Lyons. These theologians would search the Scriptures and the traditions of the Church to discover the answers to theological questions. They proclaimed what the true teaching of Christ and the Church was. The work of Christian theologians was especially important in putting down heresies, which were teachings other than those accepted by the Church.

Activity Projects

MAP ACTIVITY: CHURCH BISHOPS (*Activity Book page 192*)

1. Some bishops were more important than others because their churches were bigger and older. Locate Alexandria, Antioch, and Jerusalem and circle them with purple. The bishops of these 3 locations were very important.

2. Locate Rome and draw a yellow star on top of it. The bishop of Rome, as the successor of Peter, was (and still is) the most important bishop.

COLORING PAGE:

St. Justin Martyr (*Activity Book page 193*)

Color the picture of St. Justin Martyr just before he is killed for his faith.

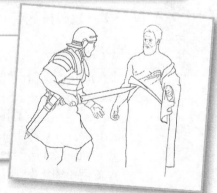

CROSSWORD PUZZLE: THE GROWTH OF THE CATHOLIC CHURCH *(Activity Book page 195)*

Across:
2. Gnostics
4. Heresy
5. Mass
7. Apologists
9. Sabellians
10. Marcionites
11. Cyprian
13. Justin
14. Donatism

Down:
1. Rome
3. Christians
6. Apology
8. Theologians
12. Synod
15. Theology

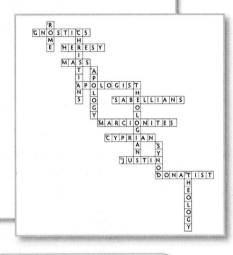

DOUBLE PUZZLE: GROWTH OF THE CATHOLIC CHURCH

(Activity Book page 196) Unscramble the words from the sections "The First Christian Apologists" and "Christian Theology." Copy the letters in the numbered blocks to the blocks with the corresponding numbers at the bottom.

CRAFT PROJECT: CATHOLIC CHURCH AND ROMAN EMPIRE TREES

Materials:
☐ Templates from the Activity Book *(Activity Book page 197–199)*
☐ 1 empty toilet paper roll
☐ Grey and brown crayons
☐ Green paint
☐ Tape
☐ Scissors
☐ Paint brush

Directions:
1. Tear out the 2 tree templates in the Activity Book.
2. Color the trunk of the slightly larger tree black indicating that it is dying.
3. Color the trunk of the smaller tree brown.
4. Cut the toilet paper roll down the middle lengthwise so that the circle in no longer complete.

5. Now make another cut down the middle lengthwise so that you have two long pieces of the roll.

6. Set one piece aside.

7. Bend the remaining piece in half and tape the edges together. Bend it so that the edge is a leaf shape.

8. Dip the edge of the toilet paper roll in the green paint and then stamp in onto the branches of the brown trunk tree. Make as many leaf stamps as will fit.

9. Using a paint brush, fill in the leaves of the tree.

10. Label the dying tree "Roman Empire" and the healthy tree "Catholic Church."

11. Enjoy!

CHAPTER 34
The Empire Divided

QUESTIONS FOR REVIEW:

1. **What did the emperor Diocletian do to the Roman Empire to try to bring more stability?**

   Divided the empire in half, east and west, and ruled it alongside a co-emperor. He also proposed that each emperor name his successor while still alive so there was no confusion concerning who would take power.

2. **Who was the well known Christian martyr killed by Diocletian?**

   Sebastian.

3. **What was the Great Persecution?**

   A time in ancient Rome under the emperor Diocletian when Christian churches were destroyed and all copies of the Bible were handed over and burned. Christians were forbidden from gathering for worship, and all bishops and clergy were imprisoned, killed, or exiled. All persons throughout the empire had to sacrifice to the Roman gods or face arrest.

4. **What set off the Great Persecution and brought about Diocletian's hatred of the Christians?**

   A Christian deacon proclaimed that the Roman gods were demons. When Diocletian's palace burned down, he blamed the Christians.

5. **Who was the young female martyr killed by the Romans for refusing to marry a wealthy Roman nobleman?**

   Agnes.

NARRATION EXERCISES:

Diocletian

He was a Greek military officer who became emperor of Rome in 285 A.D. Diocletian's family had once been slaves. He rose through the ranks of the army and by 285 had enough power to kill his opponent and proclaim himself emperor. To give the Roman Empire more stability, Diocletian divided the empire in half, east and west. He ruled the east, and his co-emperor, Maximian, ruled the west. Diocletian also realized that the empire had no stable plan of succession. Instead of fighting over succession, Diocletian said each emperor should appoint a successor while he was still alive. Taking these measures ended the civil wars in Rome. Diocletian was originally friendly to Christians and left them alone, but after a Christian deacon proclaimed that Roman gods were demons, and Diocletian's palace burned down (which he blamed on the Christians), he set off the Great Persecution, when Christians were persecuted and even put to death. In 305 A.D., after twenty years of rule and at the height of the persecution, Diocletian resigned from office and left the empire to his successor. This was the first time any Roman Emperor had ever voluntarily left office. Diocletian's legacy was one of success and a failure. One the one hand, he ended the fifty years of civil war and chaos that had almost destroyed Rome, and broke up power by dividing the empire into parts and allowing other important men to share in governing it. He also established a stable plan of succession, and won victories over barbarians. One the other hand, Diocletian failed to help the Roman economy and ruled more like a king than any emperor before him. The Senate and other institutions became useless under Diocletian and his successors. Above all else, he began the longest and worst persecution of Christians in ancient Rome.

Activity Projects

CRYPTOGRAM: DIOCLETIAN *(Activity Book page 201)*

Code chosen at random

This ordered that all Christian churches be destroyed, and all copies of the Bible be handed over and burned. Christians were forbidden from gathering for worship. All bishops and clergy were to be imprisoned and all persons throughout the empire had to sacrifice to the gods or face arrest.

Answer: The Great Persecution

CRAFT PROJECT 1: BOW AND ARROW THAT DOESN'T KILL SAINT SEBASTIAN

Materials:
- ☐ Hardwood stick of appropriate length for the student.
- ☐ Knife / chisel
- ☐ Sandpaper
- ☐ Rubber bands
- ☐ Thin wooden dowel (about the thickness of a pencil)
- ☐ Pencil eraser tops
- ☐ Hot glue

Directions:
1. Using a knife or chisel, scrape the bark from the stick.
2. Use sandpaper to smooth the stick. This will be the bow.
3. Create a slight notch at the top and bottom of the bow as grooves for the rubber bands.
4. Loop rubber bands together to make a chain as long as you will need for the length of the bow.
5. Attach the first rubber band to the top of the arrow by looping it over and over at the notch until it is firmly in place. Repeat with the last rubber band at the bottom of the arrow.
6. Cut the dowel to a 12-15 inch length.
7. Have an adult create a notch in one end of the arrow for fitting over the rubber band string.
8. Hot glue the pencil eraser top onto the other end of the arrow thus creating a blunt tip.
9. Enjoy!

CHAPTER 35
In This Sign, Conquer

QUESTIONS FOR REVIEW:

1. **Who was the emperor of the west that Constantine waged war against?**
   Maxentius.

2. **How did Constantine receive his famous vision that changed the world?**
   In a dream.

3. **What was the significance of the chi-rho symbol?**
   It was the symbol of the Christian God.

4. **What does "In hoc signo vinces" translate to, and what did it mean to Constantine?**
   It translates to "In this sign, conquer." Constantine saw it written across the sky in his dream where he had seen the symbol of the Christian God. He took this to mean he should conquer his enemy in the name of Jesus Christ.

5. **What was the Edict of Milan?**
   It was a decree issued by Constantine that legalized Christianity in Rome and restored all Christian property that had been wrongly taken.

NARRATION EXERCISE:

Constantine

He was an energetic young commander and son of the recently-deceased emperor of the west, Constantius Chlorus. Upon the death of his father, Constantine was made emperor of Britain, Gaul, and Spain. His hard work, military skill, and building projects soon won him the admiration of his subjects. But in Italy, a usurper named Maxentius had seized power and was mocking Constantine. In 313 A.D., Constantine led his army of 40,000 men from Gaul into Italy. He had success in winning some Italian towns and cities over to him, but Maxentius remained in Rome with a very large army. While strategizing about a battle plan, Constantine had a dream where the symbol of the Christian God appeared to him, along with a slogan that read "In this sign, conquer." He took this to mean the Christian God was with him, and he ordered all his soldiers to write the symbol on their shields. They were ultimately victorious in battle, and Constantine became the first Christian emperor of Rome. He enacted the Edict of Milan, which legalized Christianity and restored all Christian property that was wrongly seized. Constantine surrounded himself with Christian bishops and saints. Christians came out of the shadows and began to worship Jesus Christ publicly, giving glory to Him and thanks for the goodness of Constantine.

Activity Projects

MAP ACTIVITY: CONSTANTINE *(Activity Book page 202)*

1. Locate Gaul on the map. With red, draw a line from Gaul to Italy passing over the Alps.
2. Outside of Rome draw a tent to show that Constantine made camp outside the city to decide what his next move would be.
3. Outside of Rome, draw a shield with a chi-ro (an "x" with a "p" over it) on it. Constantine ordered all of his men to paint this symbol on their shields after having a dream in which he was told "in this sign conquer." This marked the conversion of the new Roman Emperor!

CRYPTOGRAM: THE DREAM THAT CHANGED THE WORLD

Code chosen at random

(Activity Book page 203) Constantine ordered his solders to paint the chi-rho on their shields because he saw these words appear across the symbol.

Answer: In this sign conquer

CRAFT PROJECT: CHI-RHO SHIELD - CONSTANTINE'S DREAM

Materials:
- ☐ Cardboard
- ☐ Duct tape
- ☐ Red paint
- ☐ Paint brush
- ☐ Scissors

Directions:

1. Cut your shield to desired size from the cardboard
2. Cut a 6 inch x 2 inch strip of cardboard and duct tape it as a handle to the back of your shield.
3. Paint the chi-rho symbol which looks like the letter X with a P over it.
4. Enjoy!

SNACK PROJECT: EDICT OF MILAN FEAST CELEBRATION CAKE

Imagine that you are a Christian who has lived under persecution. You have just heard of the Edict of Milan. How overjoyed you must be! Christianity is now legalized and, it is now safe to be a Christian. Christian property is being restored to those from whom it was taken. Jesus Christ can now be worshiped publicly! It's time to have a party! Follow the recipe below or create your own special feast for the occasion.

Celebration Pound Cake with Strawberries

Ingredients:
- ☐ 1 cup butter, softened
- ☐ 3 cups sugar
- ☐ 6 eggs
- ☐ 3 cups all-purpose flour
- ☐ 1/4 tsp. baking soda
- ☐ 1/4 tsp. salt
- ☐ 1 cup sour cream
- ☐ 1 tsp. vanilla extract
- ☐ 1/2 tsp. almond extract
- ☐ Confectioners' sugar
- ☐ Baking spray

Directions:

1. Preheat oven to 325 degrees.
2. In a bowl, cream the butter.
3. Beat in the sugar and continue to beat until light and fluffy (several minutes).
4. Beat in eggs one at a time.
5. Combine the dry ingredients in a separate bowl.
6. Mix the dry ingredients with the butter / sugar.
7. Gradually mix in the sour cream, vanilla, and almond.
8. Use baking spray to grease a tube pan.
9. Pour batter into the tube pan.
10. Bake for approximately 1 hour and 15 minutes (check cake after an hour as baking times may vary).
11. Allow cake to cool some in the pan before removing it to a cooling rack to completely cool.
12. Sprinkle confectioners' sugar over the top.
13. Slice and serve with fresh strawberries.
14. Enjoy!

Acknowledgments

Creating the Teacher's Manual for *The Story of Civilization* was a large project, made possible by many talented and generous people.

Thank you to the many moms, teachers, church groups, and others who generously shared their ideas and creativity. I also would like to thank the Saint Benedict Press team for all of their hard work and dedication in making this project come together, including: Mara Persic, art director; Caroline Kiser, graphic designer; Nick Vari, production editor; and Morgan Witt, editorial intern.

Lastly, I would like to thank my family for all their love and support. My children, Aiden, Mary, Patrick, Peter, Jude, Paul, Teresa, Imelda, David and Annie are a daily source of inspiration for me. Without them this book would not exist. And Conor Gallagher, my publisher, is also my husband. I love you, Conor, and am blessed beyond measure to have you as both.

 **TAN·BOOKS**

TAN Books was founded in 1967 to preserve the spiritual, intellectual and liturgical traditions of the Catholic Church. At a critical moment in history TAN kept alive the great classics of the Faith and drew many to the Church. In 2008 TAN was acquired by Saint Benedict Press. Today TAN continues its mission to a new generation of readers.

From its earliest days TAN has published a range of booklets that teach and defend the Faith. Through partnerships with organizations, apostolates, and mission-minded individuals, well over 10 million TAN booklets have been distributed.

More recently, TAN has expanded its publishing with the launch of Catholic calendars and daily planners—as well as Bibles, fiction, and multimedia products through its sister imprints Catholic Courses (CatholicCourses.com) and Saint Benedict Press (SaintBenedictPress.com). In 2015, TAN Homeschool became the latest addition to the TAN family, preserving the Faith for the next generation of Catholics (www.TANHomeschool.com).

Today TAN publishes over 500 titles in the areas of theology, prayer, devotions, doctrine, Church history, and the lives of the saints. TAN books are published in multiple languages and found throughout the world in schools, parishes, bookstores and homes.

For a free catalog, visit us online at
TANBooks.com

Or call us toll-free at
(800) 437-5876